Natasha!

Stay encourage

RESURRECTION
— *from* —
REJECTION

STEVEN EUGENE CARTER

ENDORSEMENTS

"It is a rarity for a book to speak to the head and the heart. It is certainly uncommon for a book to speak to the head and heart and touch the soul. Steven Carter's first publication masterfully weaves all three areas of learning. Steven resembles a skilled athlete standing in a triple threat position on the court of life, giving thoughtful insight, heart breaking stories and healing illustrations with a soulful touch. All who are concerned about the future of the family and institutions such as the church will do well to read this book and implement the strategies offered. No other publication in recent memory speaks to the hidden demons of rejection, anger and pain with the raw sensitivity of this book. Read it and be transformed!"

—*Reverend Otis Moss, III, Senior Pastor*
Trinity United Church of Christ
Chicago, Illinois

"Carter, in his book, proves that when an individual takes the times to evaluate themselves, they can grow into depths that they did not know were hidden inside of their reality. During his three years on staff at Brentwood, I observed him journey through his pains and challenges, and to see that he has transformed it into encouragement for others is nothing shorter than superb. I encourage anyone who ever felt rejected, isolated, abandoned or discontent with your life, to read this book and you will experience freedom if you apply the principles."

—Dr. Joe Samuel Ratliff, Senior Pastor
Brentwood Baptist Church
Houston, Texas

"Carter has taken us inside a cell of uncertainty and isolation many have no capacity to comprehend. On the one hand, he has exposed certainties many take for granted as great blessings. On the other hand, he has afforded a degree of understanding for what it is like to live without those certainties. He comes to the task with the insights of a believer and pastor. For that, he can speak bilingually in the voice of one who knows both anxiety and triumph. Steven has given voice to some who cannot speak for themselves, and he has done this noble deed with eloquence and grace, minus bitterness. Stories of triumph are needed in every generation to make it known that no matter what hand one is dealt in life, there are real possibilities for overcoming. This book has the promise of performing great service to the church and society by making us more keenly aware of the weight in choices and actions. With this work, Pastor Carter has supplied a 'Must Read' for those expecting and attempting to render relevant ministry and compassionate service."

—Dr. William Clair Turner, Jr., Professor
Duke University
Durham, North Carolina

"Profusely personal, emotionally daring, substantially practical, this written revelation of a scared, but now healed, soul will provide redemption for any deeply hurt persons who dare to delve into its bold and honest pages."

—Dr. Aaron Larry Parker, Associate Professor
Morehouse College
Atlanta, Georgia

"As a therapist, I have worked with individuals and families for more than twenty-five years. Never was there such clear and concise information given with confidence to create a sense of confidence to both counselor and counselee. If we carefully follow these principles, we will have a better chance of experiencing the resurrection that Carter chronicled on his journey. This book is about hurt, hope, faith, and freedom grounded in the understanding that there is strength in the human spirit. Everyone should read this book."

—Dr. Clive E. Neil, Psycho-Therapist
Brooklyn, New York

"Carter courageously opens up a window into his life, and takes us on a literary journey from the pain of rejection to the power of resurrection. In doing so, this book informs, inspires and instills hope in the ability to confront and overcome adversity. His story makes clear that a perceived knock-down is very different than a knock-out."

—The Honorable Hakeem Jeffries, U.S. Congressman
Eighth Congressional District, New York

"Steven Carter has written this book with a candor and passion that empowers all who have experienced any level of rejection or abandonment. He reminds us that we are what we think, and he makes a profound case for "renewing the mind" through a relationship with Christ so that feelings of low self-esteem and insecurity do not control the believer. Read it and be renewed. "

—*Drs. Floyd & Elaine Flake, Senior Pastors*
Greater Allen Cathedral AME Church
Jamaica Queens, New York

"Steven Carter graciously brings us into his own intriguing journey to wholeness. With tremendous transparency and the highest level of honesty, he helps us to face the rejection, fight the self-destruction and frees us to move on to God's preordained destination. This awesome book provides practical godly principles to rise above our painful past to reach the place God has prepared for us...achieving this by refocusing from those who have rejected us to our loving Lord and all the others whom God has strategically placed in our lives to assist in our ascension. You will be tremendously blessed by this insightful and powerful book."

—*Reverend Jeffrey Johnson, Senior Pastor*
Eastern Star Baptist Church
Indianapolis, Indiana

"Steven Carter has chronicled and catalogued his own personal faith journey with such profundity and passion in this book that anyone who reads it will be rescued, redeemed and revived by the power of God in ways that they may have never imagined. This work effectively attacks the satanic strongholds of rejection and its resultant self-destructive behavior, which are both, unfortunately, much too prevalent in the church and in the culture. This book will be a blessing to your life."

—*Dr. Jesse T. Williams, Jr., Senior Pastor*
Convent Avenue Baptist Church
Harlem, New York

"For well over 15 years, I have watched God mature Steven E. Carter as a preacher and pastor. The greater privilege, however, has been to witness him mature as a man, who is yet driven and shaped by the power of the Holy Spirit. Greater still is the gift God has permitted me to sample through reading "Resurrection from Resurrection." Carter, who preaches the gospel with passion and joy, has written a book which evidences—to borrow the words of the mystic Dr. Howard Thurman—"pain has a ministry." With admirable courage, Rev. Carter offers his story, with the lessons he has learned, as a Christ-centered message of hope and model of healing."

—*Reverend Anthony L. Trufant, Senior Pastor*
Emmanuel Baptist Church
Brooklyn, New York

"In his book, Resurrection from Rejection, Steven Carter is transparent and transformative, as he guides those who are stuck in the pit of unhealthy responses to rejection to the mountain top of personal acceptance. Read what Pastor Carter has to say, and allow God to set you free."

—**Dr. Maurice Watson, Senior Pastor**
Beulahland Bible Church
Macon, Georgia

"'Resurrection from Rejection' is an incredible story that will uplift the minds and souls of its readers. He uniquely reveals his deepest personal pains to detail important lessons to all who venture into this journey. As a leader in New York City, I am proud to be his friend and grateful for everything he has taught me in how to be a better person."

—**Jeffrey Maddrey, Deputy Chief**
New York City Police Department

Resurrection from Rejection: Healing From 7 Areas of Rejection in Your Life
by Steven E. Carter

© 2014 by Steven E. Carter

All rights reserved.

Steven E. Carter
P.O. Box 208
Bayonne, NJ, 07002

Phone: 281.891.3653
Fax: 718.228.8355

International Standard Book Number: 978-1-940786-09-4

Library of Congress Catalogue Card Number: Available Upon Request

Printed in the United States of America

First Edition, May, 2014

Trademarks

TABLE *of* CONTENTS

FOREWORD
DR. RALPH DOUGLAS "PAS" WEST

There is a new weekly series named, *RESURRECTION*. I'm taking bets with myself on how long the show will last. I haven't looked at it because it sounds rather weird. From what I can gather from the advertisement, it has something to do with people who come back from the dead. But the living loved ones who have moved on with their lives are confronted with loved ones who have been resurrected and they are living life asking one question, "Are you alive or are you dead?"

There is something about comebacks that intrigue many of us; whether it is our favorite sports team trailing for the majority of the game who surges on to win in a dramatic fashion or to see someone who has taken a moral fall or an ethical failure rebound and make a comeback. I can scarcely contain myself when I see Michael Vick take the football field and throw a pass, pick six, or make a touchdown…it doesn't matter; he is the embodiment of someone who has made a comeback.

Resurrection from Rejection is the autobiographical odyssey of Steven Carter – rejected at birth, adopted as an infant by a benevolent mother and father, despite the knowledge of the possibility of little Steven not living to experience his first birthday. Then growing up in the Carter's home, where his father modeled before him what it means to be a MAN. Now that sickly little boy has grown up to be one of the most responsible and respected religious figures in the Borough of Brooklyn, New York.

I have had the privilege of knowing Steve for more than a decade now. He has entrusted me with his most intimate joys and pains regarding his adoption. I listened to Steve as he agonized over being rejected by his birth parents. But I have learned to listen to him tell his story without trying to edit it. Rejection often reminds me that there was a good man named Job who lived in the land of Uz. He was a man of who loved God and hated evil, a man of means and a father of many children. In one day, his paradise gain was turned into paradise lost. He found himself sitting in the ashes questioning how bad things could happen to good people. While he sat in the ashes he was surrounded by friends who attempted to correct him, rather than merely listen to him, and participate in his proverbs from the ashes. Then in some redemptive way, he made a comeback.

My gift to Steve may be the one you find yourself giving to him while reading his story, which is the gift of listening to him without attempting to edit the painful moments of his life. Neither did I try to give him a panacea for his long journey into the light. For I have learned it is upon the anvil of difficulty that life takes the mallet to hammer out something beautiful.

Resurrection from Rejection is not a story of morbidity.

"We did not dare to breathe a prayer,
Or give our anguish scope.
Something was dead within us,
And what was dead was Hope."
Oscar Wilde, *The Ballad of Reading Gaol*

Resurrection from Rejection is the story of Hope. Steve dares to breath a prayer and gives his aguish scope. There is nothing dead within him, what is alive is HOPE.

The readers will find themselves on an emotional roller coaster. Sometimes they will laugh at the stories Steven tells. Other times the reader will cry as he holds up a mirror and you catch the reflection of rejection from your own story within his story. And still other times you might sense the brimstone burning within you as you reflect with the author as he conjures up some unresolved rejection you, too, have rendezvoused. But most of all, you will rejoice as he takes you by the hand and escorts you to his own happy resolve. One thing is true…it has taken all of these events, experiences and episodes to shape the life and philosophy of Steven Carter.

Maybe I'll go On Demand and look at the first episodes of *RESURRECTION* and see what all the hype is about. I do love a good comeback story. Admittedly, watching the underdog win is euphoric.

BUT if I don't, I'll pull out my New Testament and read the story of the greatest of all comebacks!

—Dr. Ralph Douglas "Pas" West
The Church Without Walls
Houston, Texas

ACKNOWLEDGEMENTS

One of the greatest challenges in writing this book was thinking of the people to express my gratitude to. There are so many individuals who played a part in making this book a reality. I have been blessed with so many wonderful people in my life who have made a great impact on my life that trying to name everyone, living or deceased, is a task beyond my ability or memory. However, I will make an attempt to express my gratitude to several individuals.

To my lovely wife, Danielle Marie Carter

My angel, my lover, my wife, my partner and my best friend. Thanks for marrying me and giving up so much to help me become more of what God called me to be. You have taken me to heights I never knew existed and you helped me see possibilities I never dreamed of. Thank you for believing in me and encouraging me to finish this book when I felt like giving up. I thank you for the hours you spent reading every page and catching errors that I did not see. Not one time did you tell me you were tired, you kept saying, *"Let's make this a huge success and tell your story to help others."* I wake up every morning feeling like the luckiest man in the world. When you would say little things to me like, *"You can really help people with this book." "I believe in you and the power of your story." "Don't write it if you are not going to be real, people deserve the truth,"* and so many other words of encouragement, you added to me the extra zeal that I needed to continue pursuing my goal. I say without any equivocation, this project could not have been completed without your perpetual inspiration. Thank you also for being patient with me in my healing process, and I know I still have a long journey ahead. Outside of having a relationship with God, you are my greatest JOY! I love you and there is nothing you can do about it. You and I will always be an example of what it means when God brings two individuals together for a purpose greater than the both of them can see. In the words of the classic song, *"If loving you is wrong, I don't want to be right."*

To My Wonderful Parents

The both of you made it possible for me to write this book. The both of you loved me when everyone else gave me up, and I am ever indebted. Only God could have sent such parents my way, and I am glad God allowed me to be passed up by others so that I could be accepted by the both of you. I love the both of you for all of your sacrifices, lessons, chastisement, encouragement, and everything that you instilled in my life. I am where I am today and who I am because of the both of you. Love you always Dad & Ma!

To My Family

My life could not be what it is without the special people who God blessed me to be able to call my family. I could name many, but I want to give a special appreciation to *Aunt Hester, Uncle William (Deceased), Uncle Jimmy, Aunt Rose, Uncle Moses, Aunt Francis, Uncle George (Deceased), Uncle John (Deceased), Uncle Lincoln (Deceased), Aunt Margie (Deceased), Uncle Melvin, Aunt Mary, Aunt Jean, Uncle Billy, Aunt Vernetta (Deceased),*

Grandma Fannie Powell (Deceased), Grandma Ellen Glover (Deceased), Uncle Junior (Deceased), Aunt Ceila Mae, Aunt Annette, Uncle Vernon, Auntie Bell, Aunt Lizzie Harrington (Deceased), Mae Washington (Deceased), Uncle Charlie, Aunt Elenora, and so many more. I can't leave out my cousins *Teresa (like a sister), Paul, Vanessa, Patricia, Atiya, Kajuan, Khadiya, Alicia, Tyeisha, Tony, Dawn (like a sister), William, II; Virgil, Vern, Valerie, Sharon, Kevis, Marcus, Carla, Terry, Kevin,* and so many more. Thank each and every one of you, in some way you have played a role in helping me to become who I am today, and I will forever love you for it

To My In-Laws & Friends

Thank you for accepting me into your family with unconditional love. I have grown to see the closeness that each of you share, and it has made me ever so happy to know that you have allowed me to become one of the many who are privileged to be a part of this family. Special thanks to *Ma Cathy, Poppa John, Derek & Tijuana, Monique, Lil Derek, Kye & Laurynn, Lodric, Shannon & Julie, Dedric & Traneka, Monte (Smooth Brother), A'frica & Jon, Shatona, Precious, Kim & Dyshon, Joseph Earle, Cynthia Patterson, Taylor, Kirby,* and so many others. Each of you is loved in a special way by my wife, and because each of you mean so much to her, each of you is truly valued and loved in my heart. Thanks for welcoming me in as if I have always been a part of your lives.

To Dr. Elliott & Mrs. Virginia Cuff

There is nothing for me to say other than, "I love the both of you more than words can ever express." You were there to encourage me to spread my wings and become someone in life. I remember the words to this day, "Steven, the sky is the limit. You are the only one who can cause failure in your life." Thanks a million for helping me believe in myself and move beyond countless obstacles that were both visible and invisible. The both of you served as my springboard into the deep waters of life and discovery; and because of your love and patience, I did not drown, but was able to float on the waters of faith and land on many great shores of life. I can never repay each of you for your investments, but I can promise that I will always live out the principles that you imparted to me. When I think about the many sacrifices you made as if I was a child from your womb or lineage, it makes my heart fill up with joy and gladness. I am ever indebted to you and will always remain as a mark of your investment in building up another servant to take the Word of God to all people in all places.

To Dr. Joe Samuel & Mrs. Doris Ratliff

Special thanks to Dr. Joe Samuel Ratliff and the Brentwood Baptist Church who helped me learn more about ministry than seminary could have ever taught me. Dr. Ratliff, you are one of the greatest mentors that any person in ministry could ever desire. I will always be indebted to you for taking me with no experience and allowing me to learn, at your expense, and prepare myself for ministry. May God continue to favor you and Mrs. Ratliff as the both of you bless so many people across this country. Always know that you, Sister Doris Ratliff, The Dream Team (Kevin Williams, Lillie Seals, Carolyn Pickens, Barbara Thomas, Paul Jefferson, Tena Davis, Deborah Jordan, Augustus Green, Joseph Ford, Angela Green, Mrs. Scott), and the Brentwood Church family will always remain special in my heart. Thanks for everything.

To Dr. Ralph Douglas & Mrs. Sheretta West

This book was birthed out of a casual conversation that you shared with me during a visit to New York. More details of the conversation are in the book; therefore, I want to say, "Thanks." Thank you, Mrs. West, affectionately known as "Aunt Ree," for sharing your husband with me and so many others across this country. Thank you for allowing me to become more than just a young preacher, but allowing me to become a part of the "West" Family. Thank you for never being too busy to answer my calls regardless of the time of day or night. Thank you for listening to me even when it seems like you have told me the same thing more than once, twice or even three times. Let me also express my sincere gratitude to Ralph, Ralpheal & Rennekia who have allowed me to share your space of intimacy with your father. I love all of you dearly and may God continue to smile upon your present and your future.

To Pastors Michael Walrond & Dr. LaKeesha Walrond

I will never forget how the both of you welcomed me into your family during my seminary years at Duke. Mike, I learned so much from observing you and listening to you. You were always considered one of the greatest Chapel Assistants to serve at Morehouse College, and I was privileged to serve with you during your time at Zion Hill United Church of Christ. Now that we are serving in the same state (New York) and celebrating the same anniversary, life truly has a way of keeping people connected. Thank you for taking time out to help me walk through some insightful thoughts during the development of this manuscript. May God continue to bless you as you continue to make a huge impact on so many lives in Harlem, New York, as you serve faithfully at First Corinthian Baptist Church. Again, thanks for helping this young seminarian out.

To Mount Ararat Church

Thank you to every leader and member who stands with me. I thank each of you for your patience as I have been writing this book. To be able to serve as leader of the ministry where I was raised was never an idea in my mind, but I am so glad that God led me home. I would rather be no other place. I love each of you and without you and your patience, I would not have been able to complete this book. May we continue to grow together as Pastor & People. Special thanks to *Lula Walker, Geraldine Campbell, Carrie Richardson, Ethel Nicholson, Charles Crawley, Willie Zellars, Andre Lennon, Genese Morgan, Bella Joseph, Cedric Gaddy, Richard Bramwell, Nadia Rhodes, Stacey Starkes, George Brown, Duane Harris (Deceased), Melvin Talley, Milton Bullock, Richard Durham, Kenny Ade, Sandra Scott, Juanita Dingle, Mary Paul, Simon Tillery, Patricia Wingate, Darlene Wilson, Juanita Kelly, Janet Bullock (my 1st and only Daughter-In-Ministry), Maurice Perry, Kywani Wade, Kim Summerson, Kajawan Sulton, Phil Weatherspoon, Stanley Brown (Music Ministry Consultant), Wayne Walker, Nedra Natal, Taneka Simone, Travis Wade, Patricia Price, Tamika Jones Fernandez, Karla Walters, Jackie Fuller, Kiana Terry* and many others. Every name above has in some way or another played a role in the successes we have experienced at Mount Ararat, and I am thankful to each of you.

To all of my Co-Laborers

There are many pastors who have allowed me over the years to come and stand behind their sacred desk to proclaim the Word of God. I am ever so thankful because they could have sent the invitations to others. Here are just a few names that I am thankful for, and know that there are many others. Pastors such as *Dr. Johnny Ray Youngblood, James C. Perkins, Floyd & Elaine Flake, Otis Moss, Jr., Otis Moss, III, Cynthia Hale, Maurice Watson,*

Frederick D. Haynes, III, William Franklin Richardson, Dwight Jones, Sr.,
Dwight Jones, Jr., Gary Faulkner, Terrance Johnson, Solomon Kinloch, Jawanza
K. Colvin, Delman Coates, Lawrence Aker, Shaun Jerry Lee, Claybon Lea,
Clinton Miller, The Late William Augustus Jones, Gary V. Simpson, Vernon
Walton, Lester Taylor, Marquette Peace, Anthony Trufant, DeQuincy Hentz,
Aaron Parker, Kevin Johnson, Calvin O. Butts, Paul Dunn, David Hampton,
Darran Mitchell, A. Louis Patterson, Prince Rivers, Akin Royal, Dennis Hebert,
Ziddie Hamatheite, Washington L. Lundy, Curtis L. Whitney, The Late
Dwight M. Jackson, Reginald L. Bachus, The Late H. Devore Chapman, Lee P.
Washington, Matthew Whatley, Joe Carter, Clarence Norman, Daryl Bloodsaw,
David Kelley, Gerald Kisner, Lawrence Edward Carter, Sr., Kevin Jones, Craig
Brown, Calvin Rice, Paul Dunn, Howard John Wesley, Marcus King, William
Hartsdale, Reginald Jones, Lisa Jenkins, David Brawley, Jesse Williams, Leonzo
Lynch, A.L. Jinwright, Alan Patterson, Terrance McKinley, Samuel Bullock,
David Bullock and so many others whose names I cannot all submit. I want
to thank you for allowing me to live out my calling through your pulpits
across this nation.

To Dr. D. Daryl Griffin

Hey man, how can I thank you? You reminded me that I have a story
to tell. Do you remember when you gave me this long speech? Let me
just summarize it. *"Steven, you have to get this message out. The enemy tried to*
destroy your life from birth because he knew you would make a great impact. Now
you have to put it in print so that you can have a story that will be immortal and
reach the world and show the enemy he did not win." Those words hit me like
a hard baseball bat, and I thank you for it. That day I was encouraged to
keep on writing and I did not stop until I was finished. Thanks a million
man, you never know how one conversation can add value to someone's

life. Keep on speaking encouraging words to the people you lead and the best is yet to come.

To Sundi Lofty

I have never really told you, but thanks for sharing the story of adoption with me about your family. Being able to KNOW that there are others out there who have successfully navigated through the terrains of feeling rejected has served as a goal of mine. I want you to personally know that your story played a role in helping me realize that being adopted is not a burden, but is really a blessing in disguise. Please continue to share your story with those who desire to listen and hear the power of what happens when a family takes someone in and loves them as their own. I know without ever speaking to your brother, that his life is all the better because of the way your mother and your family loved him. Thank you sister, I will never forget the many conversations.

Deputy Chief Jeffrey Maddrey

Thank you for being an example to me about moving forward. Having the privilege of seeing you continue to reach higher ranks in the New York City Police Department showed me that as a young African-American man, I can excel to great heights. Your successes have encouraged me along the way. Your leadership in the community where I serve has always proven to me that if you love people, people will love you. It is not often that people in your profession are loved, but I have seen people gravitate towards you because of the way you put the needs of the people in front, and at many times I have seen you put them in front of your personal and family obligations, which I am certain was only allowed because of the loving wife (Helen) and children you have. In addition, allowing my family to be connected with your family has proven nothing but happiness. You have always celebrated with me in various ways, and I will always be thankful to you for your words of encouragement. May God continue to bless you as He moves you to higher levels in your career with the New York City Police Department.

To My Many Encouragers

There are so many friends who have been a blessing in my life and have helped me come to this process, and I am ever so appreciative. People such as *Shanel Cooper Imonite (gave me the title), Chuck & Nandi Welch, Teri Johnson, Rani Johnson, Don & Lisa Williams, Odell & Chris Winn, Victor Singletary (Editor), Larence Snowden, Jarrod & Porshea Wilkins, Chris & Karen Bramwell, Ibrahim Parham, Andre Humphrey, Terrance Fontaine, Ronald & Hillary Green, Larry Green, Mr. & Mrs. Harry Johnson, Ethel Johnson, Anthony Merriweather, Anthony Vanputter, Michael Cooper, Aja Nichols, Krista Kerin,* and so many others.

PREFACE

BREAKING NEWS!

Have you ever felt *violated, betrayed, neglected, insecure, depressed, abandoned, unhappy, useless, lonely, worthless, hopeless, hurt, angry, bitter, wounded, invisible, belittled, unwanted, withdrawn, or as if the world was against you?* If so, you have picked up the right book. These feelings and more became real to me at a very young age. At thirteen years old, I was home one day with my mother and my aunt. It was an average day in the life of a typical adolescent. I do not recall anything particular about the weather, the setting or some other major current event. Yet, what began as an ordinary day became the day I learned the true meaning of the word, irreversible. In the midst of their conversation, my mother paused to tell me to take the trash out. Occupied with adolescent busyness, I responded that I would but I did not move immediately. After a delay, my aunt said to me, "You should always move when they call you because they did not have to adopt you." Puzzled, I looked at my mother who said, "Steven pay no attention to her, just take out the trash." In that instant exchange, my aunt's well-intentioned, but very poorly timed, words irreversibly removed the veil of a longstanding family and personal secret. I was adopted!

Devout religious persons, alcoholics and well-intentioned people share the regrettable character defect of saying the right thing at the perfectly wrong time. Admittedly, I needed to know someday that I am an adopted child for medical, relational, legal and other personal reasons. I, however, did not need to discover this complex and mixed truth in such a callously indifferent way. My aunt's revelation began a twenty-five year entombment and descent into personal rejection, anger, bewilderment, internal strife, emotional turmoil, loss of identity, distrust of everyone and an inability to rebound from the devastating news of my adoption. Actually, at that moment I felt like the trash that I was asked to take out. Decades later as I write, I can recall vividly the shock and horror that filled my mind and heart to learn that I was not a "real" member of my family. Everything I held sacred seemingly evaporated. I did not know whether I could trust my parents and their attestations of love and encouragement. Am I their son or am I a charity case which completed their family and established and personified their good name? How will I know whether anyone loves me unconditionally? Will anyone love Steven because he is uniquely Steven and not a personified project of which his parents assumed custody at birth? Did the rest of my extended family share my aunt's feelings that I should live my life in obsequious gratitude for the favor of having been adopted? Have they always seen me as an "outsider" who is not really a member of the family but is given a seat because of his parents' benevolence? Whereas those questions explored my rightful place, or lack thereof, in my formative and extended family, the primary question remained, "How could my birth parents have rejected me in the first place and put me up for adoption? Did they discard me like the trash that I was asked to take outside?"

Within the intervening years of the next quarter century, I would live with that primary question on a daily basis. My attempts were to answer all of these mysteries with the hope of finding a permanent and irreversible identity which no one could steal from me. I fought to define my personal and inherent worth with total disregard of the choices and words of other people, relatives or not. Essentially, the internal battle I waged correlated with a lifelong campaign to overcome the rejection I felt upon learning that I am adopted. I became hypersensitive to betrayal and deceit. I now realize that my parents consistently waited for the right time to tell me. But, their delay, undergirded by their heartfelt hopes to spare me the pain and agony which I inevitably experienced, felt like a huge and unforgivable betrayal upon my discovery of being adopted. The family "secret" equaled a deliberate, orchestrated and collective campaign to deceive me while everyone pitied Steven and watched from a distance to determine whether he possessed any gratefulness for his parents favor. Did anyone in the extended circle of my family and friends genuinely care about the wholesale loss of my naiveté and innocence relating to being loved and nurtured unconditionally? As a rejected person, I fulfilled the expectations anyone had of an outcast. I resisted being grateful, isolated myself and fueled my bitter and venomous anger. As my rejection complex progressed emotionally, thereby poisoning every relationship I had, and petrified within my heart creating a continual "me against the world" conflict, I withdrew further and further into the tomb of my emotional and existential death.

YOU CANNOT CHOOSE YOUR FAMILY!

Another important revelation evolved as I accepted the loss of my naiveté relating to my family. No one chooses his family. Loneliness inevitably ensues when you also realize that your family did not choose you. I began to feel as if I were Robinson Crusoe stranded on a deserted island. Yet, I accept Donne's enduring aphorism, "No man is an island, entire of itself."1 Loneliness initially appears safe and predictable. No one can hurt you if you are alone. Still, we need companionship; we are not meant to live in isolation. In synthesizing the complexity of the providential circumstances that led to my placement within my family, I am grateful for God's mysterious and mystical hand in orchestrating a place where I would receive His unconditional and unfailing love, albeit through very genuine but human beings.

By God's grace, I have experienced resurrection from my debilitating rejection during my formative years and upbringing. In this book, written through the prism of my personal burden and blessing of discovering and appreciating I am a beloved, adopted son, I offer my journey as a source of healing and inspiration to anyone experiencing rejection of any type. I seek to help and encourage individuals as they resolve issues of abandonment, failed relationships, vengeance, anger, injustice, isolation and other emotions and eventualities resulting primarily from rejection. These complex feelings and experiences paralyze many people, thereby causing them to fail in defining their primary purpose, satisfying their heart's deepest desires and fulfilling their destiny. Had I been able to surmount my rejection complex and identity crisis earlier in my life, I would have avoided countless personal and relational mistakes.

Although I may not have made the best decisions, I do not regret my choices as they afforded me lifelong lessons, which encourage and empower me as I establish better relationships and mature as a giver and recipient of genuine love. Though I write as an adopted son, I hope this book helps anyone who struggles with rejection in any aspect of life. There are as many types of rejection as there are persons experiencing this fierce, demeaning, dehumanizing and debilitating emotion. I fear for anyone battling abandonment that is unaware of his internal suffering. His pain becomes patterns of thought in his consciousness and behavior in his character that create resistance to his growth and good. Consequently, his daily physical existence converts into an entombment where he observes the death of his love, dreams, creativity, joy, happiness, peace and liberty. Anger and a myriad of other lethal emotions consistently corrode his mind, heart and soul. Humbly, I hope my story helps in resurrecting anyone whose circumstances interred him in the graveyard of rejection.

Beyond the formal definitions of rejection officially rendered by the Oxford English or Merriam Webster dictionaries, I prefer to characterize this phenomenon in practical and experiential terms instead of clinical or medical ones. *In its simplest form, rejection is a denial of the inherent and invaluable worth, dignity and unique personality of any individual.* For twenty-two years, I relegated my birth parents' decision to place me up for adoption as an unequivocal rejection of my divine uniqueness as a child of God. Personally, I considered their action equivalent with a wholesale denial of my God given talents, natural abilities and potential. They did not care enough to commit to nurturing my personality and the skills and possibilities that would unfold in my life; they rejected me. Everyone hates rejection because it ultimately means someone does not care enough to invest time, talent, treasure and temperament in your personal development. Whether prejudicial or uninformed, someone determines you simply are not worth it. Each spring, thousands of aspirants to college receive rejection letters that deeply wound their hearts as they are told their skills and intelligence do not qualify them to study at the school of their choice. Dating and refusal of romantic and sexual overtures are fraught with many levels of rejection. At a dance club, many a man becomes extremely angry when the woman who just denied his request for a dance turns to accept another man's hand. A friend of mine retains an emotional scar when he recalls his mother recoiling and shoving him away when he attempted to kiss her out of sheer excitement. Conceivably, his mother was irritated on that July day but her verbal and physical dismissal of her son, my friend, materialized into a heartfelt and bewildering rejection he carried for many years. No one appreciates denials of mortgage applications and requests for increases of credit limits, even when hard numbers simply would not justify approval. Still, we consider these denials as assaults on our character. Summarily, rejection wounds our whole being – mind, heart, body, soul, will, psyche and spirit – because it disregards the essence of our character.

RESURRECTION CAN HAPPEN IN YOUR LIFE

Resurrection is the process of revitalization that heals deep-seated personal and past wounds, thereby enabling a rejected person to actualize his potential, fulfill his dreams and goals, accomplish his destiny and experience, fully and freely, the gift of his unique God-given life. Awakening one morning to genuine self-acceptance, self-approval, self-expression and self-love are the practical evidence of having been recalled to life out of the entombment of rejection. Through daily experiences of overcoming pain and rejection in its many forms, a person experiences resurrection from rejection. Beyond Moses' encounter with a burning bush, rejected persons have healing conversations with loved ones and close friends, transform terminations into opportunities, utilize failed relationships as pathways to personal growth, and reflect upon God's mysterious ways of embedding unconditional love in the hearts of beloved adopted parents. These multidimensional epiphanies cumulatively yield resurrection from rejection.

I exhort and emphasize the necessity of committing to a process of healing and resurrection. I do not know of any easy, quick, painless or economical way to experience resurrection from rejection. Anyone seeking permanent healing from his pain must travel through the valley of the shadow of death. He must live with the dread and foreboding feeling that he may never be free of his pain. His willingness to embrace and confront his pain is the primary step of his healing process. The chemical and pharmaceutical industries are unable to supply him with a pill that erases his pain. The wizards of Madison Avenue in New York City, power players of K Street in Washington DC, writers in Hollywood, and gurus of commercial spirituality…ALL are equally powerless to assist him in avoiding the difficult, but rewarding, journey through forgiveness, self-evaluation, acceptance, denial, pain and rejuvenation. Counseling, genuine spirituality, spiritual direction, love, affirmation and an encouraging and empowering community are components of this process.

Genuinely, I hope anyone suffering with rejection will commit to acquiring and accepting a better life. You cannot change the past, but you can determine your future. Releasing your past pain and hurt is the first step in healing. As you let it go, you lessen its power over your emotions, heart and life. I put my trust in Almighty God and a few persons who loved me unconditionally. Our exchange of ideas, feelings and opinions greatly aided me in making necessary changes. You cannot expect your life to become better if you are unwilling to change. Change your impression of yourself. Change your view of other people. Again, the lens of forgiveness radically alters a person's opinion of other people. Change how you live each day. Choose healing instead of remaining entombed in an existential death of rejection. Lastly, healing necessitates resilience, as the process of zigzagging toward and around growth often tempts a person to abandon the process. However, each disappointment offers energy, and if harnessed, actually propels you further in your spiritual and personal development. Resilience results in renewal.

Unrequited love is the hardest type of rejection. It requires the longest period of healing. It is most grievous to the human heart and soul to love someone who is incapable, unwilling or uninterested in reciprocating your affection and adoration. Broken engagements, infidelity and divorce are natural outgrowths of unrequited love. Inexplicable and accordingly limitless, unrequited love petrifies into rejection because there is nothing its victims can do to resolve it. You cannot make someone love or like you; either he or she does or does not. Countless changes to your personality and adaptations to your lifestyle will not convince anyone to alter his or her opinion of you. Appearing to be someone who you are not only worsens the situation; your lack of integrity and authenticity repulses other people, particularly someone you deeply and intimately desire. However honest their refusal of your wish for a more meaningful and beloved relationship, you receive it as a rejection of you as you resolve they did not take time to know you. This especially hurtful type of rejection causes long-term pain which, left unhealed, seals the entrance of your tomb.

ARE YOU WILLING TO ACCEPT YOURSELF IN SPITE OF?

Genuine self-acceptance, self-approval, self-expression and self-love are the cure to unrequited love, specifically, and any other kind of rejection, generally. Seeing yourself as Almighty God sees you; realizing that you are "fearfully [awesomely] and wonderfully [majestically and magnificently] made in the image of Almighty God" (Psalm 139:13-16, *The Amplified Bible*), heals lingering pain and hurt of rejection. Holistically appreciating yourself is the practical means of resurrection from rejection.

As you willingly embrace the arduous, lengthy, challenging, yet rewarding and renewing process of emotional, mental, psychological and spiritual healing, you will discover new experiences, joys and mysteries in life. The door to your tomb will open and God will recall you to new life. My story and this book intend to encourage and empower individuals to move from self-rejection to self-acceptance. You cannot expect your life to become better if you are unwilling to make concrete and comprehensive changes. Fundamentally, change how you view yourself. As you commit to the painstaking and long-term work of self-acceptance, approval, love and expression, God resurrects you.

Try as hard as we may, everyone experiences some type of rejection in the seven major dimensions of life. Rightly, no one likes rejection and people overwhelmingly hate it. Self- rejection emerges from the cumulative rejection of other people. Take a snapshot of your current self-image. Do you accept, approve, esteem, express and love yourself? Do you need other people's consent to feel good about yourself? Do you always need to consult with someone else before you can solidify your opinion? Do you need a majority vote of a committee to determine what you believe and what action you will take? Second, do you still suffer with lingering emotional and personal complexes originating in your childhood formative years and family of origins? The inability or unwillingness of parents and siblings to recognize and celebrate a person's uniqueness often contributes significantly to patterns of thoughts in his consciousness and behavior in his character that create resistance to his growth. Such a person finds himself fighting battles with people on the job, in his church and within his community who remind him of his family members. Their failure to appreciate him unconditionally becomes a heartfelt rejection which unsurprisingly spills over into every relationship he forms whether professional or personal. In the concepts of Jung, a man's shadow forms as he develops a pattern of self-sabotaging behavior in reaction to his parents' and siblings' rejection.2 As he lives within the dark side of his character, he prevents himself from establishing mutually beneficial and respectful relationships as he constantly disdains the rejection of his primary caretakers and siblings. Third, naturally this dejected man experiences betrayal and disappointment from his friends, thereby compounding the pain and heartache visited upon him by his family. Seeking affirmation outside of his destructive family unit, he finds, yet again, the self-fulfilling prophecy of denial of his inherent worth and distinctive personality as he realizes his "friends" merely sieved off of his talents and loyalty. Further intensifying his pain, fourth, he experiences repeated rejections in his attempts to relate romantically and intimately with someone. He suffices as a brother, adviser, fellow sufferer, classmate and platonic friend. But whereas a woman he admires welcomes his compassion, counsel, gifts and time, she fails to reciprocate his intense emotions, equal his commitment or offer physical intimacy. This unrequited love creates an identity crisis as he longs to know who will love him unconditionally. Fifth, any termination of employment, whether deserved or not, yields the question, "Does anyone really appreciate me?" Cumulatively, these foregoing experiences of rejection lead to a fundamental crisis in faith. "Am I living a cruel joke? Has my Heavenly Father rejected me, given His allowance of years of denial, disgrace, defeat and despair?" Job asked God if He had eyes of flesh and saw as a human does. Possibly, feeling rejected by *God* lies at the heart of every type of rejection. Resolving this foremost question is the essence of resurrection from rejection.

WHAT TO EXPECT FROM MY STORY

In telling my story of adoption, rejection and recreation, I will be frank without being offensive. I will relay the raw and unvarnished details about the truth of my adoption and the internal strife I experienced subsequently. I offer no apology for sharing my story in such a forthright way. Undoubtedly, you are most familiar with the biblical adage, "You shall know the truth and the truth shall set you free," (John 8:32). Grappling with hard details, difficult facts, complex choices and very human personalities was essential to my healing process. Avoidance would not have helped me; actually, it may have enticed me with some type of addiction or other escapist approach. To heal and experience resurrection from rejection, I had to face my deepest fears and confront the reality that I am a beloved, yet adopted, son. I could not avoid a non-negotiable and arduous process of discarding my naiveté about my parents' "pure and unconditional" love through my thirteenth birthday; negating the love I had received, as I considered it suspect with the revelation of my adoption, and synthesizing my receipt of their love, as I understood love through adoption as God's plan for my life. My personal journey has been agonizing and hurtful. I share it to help anyone who struggles with rejection. I cannot do so effectively if I whitewash the pain and misery of healing from rejection. My story includes familiar intrigue and motifs of anger, conflict, romance, betrayal, isolation, resolution and reconciliation. I will not paint with broad brushstrokes, but I will not gloss over the scars, wounds, and deep ridges of pain either. Adoption is a very complex choice for all persons whom it affects. Hollywood images with sappy movies, like *Immediate Family* starring Glenn Close and James Woods, lead everyone to believe that adopted parents, children and their extended families all live happily ever after. Television public service announcements equally magnify this heartwarming myth. Neither depiction reveals the rejection that infertile prospective parents feel. Movies and commercials do not share the perplexity of teenage mothers who want to believe truly that they can rear their children, even though they know that adoption by mature, professional and financially capable adults is best for the child. In telling my story, I divulge the panorama of the adoption experience, though I concentrate meticulously upon emotions and trials of parents and children without mincing words or varnishing details.

As a pastor and minister of the Christian gospel, if I were to believe that God rejects anyone, I would resign my ordination and choose another profession. It makes sense, however, that countless persons experiencing rejection have suffered so long that they uncritically accept this misconception. In formal theological terms, we characterize this idea as heresy, an erroneous and deliberate teaching about the nature of God that contradicts His revealed character in the Person of Jesus Christ, the Holy Scriptures, history, tradition and reason. The Bible teaches that Almighty God creates each person uniquely in His image (Psalm 8 and Psalm 139). Were God to deny anyone, He must deny Himself as each person reflects His love, grace, mercy, peace and character. Still, it is hard to agree with this truth when you feel God indifferently allows limitless pain and suffering in your life. "Life's but a walking shadow, a poor player; that struts and frets his hour upon the stage; And then is heard no more. It is a tale, told by an idiot, full of sound and fury, signifying nothing" (William Shakespeare, *Macbeth* Act 5, Scene 5, Lines 20-25). Admittedly, I sympathize with this point of view, but I also know the power of God to bring someone to new life. I affirm anyone's right to ask very hard questions about faith in God. I have asked many of my own. After your final question, please listen for a response, which God graciously and lovingly gives. My story captures my experience of wrestling with the idea of unconditional love, cloaked within rejection, denial, deceit and betrayal. By God's grace, I resisted bitterness and cynicism. In so doing, I ironically learned that God's unconditional love extends beyond human delineations of biology, legacy, genealogy, tradition and heritage. Two people who share absolutely nothing in common with a newborn infant can leave a hospital with him and love him as if he were their biological child. Similarly, that infant, through the love, nurture and affirmation he receives from his parents, grows to love them as fiercely and unconditionally as if they were his biological parents. Simply stated, I learned that love emerges within a genuine relationship. As children of God, we experience His unconditional love for us in the context of a loyal, enduring, unfailing and mutually faithful relationship. Accordingly, I do not subscribe to the negative and distrustful idea that God plays cruel jokes on anyone. His trustworthy and steadfast love resurrects us each time we experience existential death.

HEALING IS POSSIBLE FOR YOU

As I do not consider it a coincidence that you are reading this book, I hope it will play a pivotal and providential role in your process of healing, encouragement and resurrection. Humbly, I ask you to finish the book... however long it may take you to do so. Travel with me through the prism of my experience. Walk beside me as I traverse, in hindsight, the tough terrain of emotions and experiences resulting in my entombment to rejection. Mystically, return with me to the sight of my resurrection. Chances are my story includes similar scenes, plot twists, characters, settings, conflicts, dilemmas and themes in your personal drama. I suspect we have dealt with the same issues relating to rejection. Fortuitously, observing the antecedents, causes, developments and resolutions of my pain will encourage and empower you as you heal from your own pain. Personalize your observations of my experience. God is not a respecter of persons. What He did in my life, He will accomplish equally, and perhaps more powerfully, in your life!

Healing from rejection occurs as you irreversibly cultivate self-acceptance (inclusive of self-approval and self-love) and self-expression, the surest antidotes to any type of rejection. As you clearly and securely define who you are, you are less likely to experience rejection. Self-acceptance reduces the need for external affirmation and acceptance. As this trait increases as an intrinsic attribute of your character, you equally, irreversibly release the need for other people's approval. As you no longer need other people's approval and their opinions become right-sized in your thinking, you feel less rejected by others because they can no longer determine your worth. As you let go of other people's opinions, you also forgive their incapacities, particularly your parents' and siblings' character defects. Forgiveness opens your eyes to the imperfections of other people, even those persons whom you love. As you learn to love them despite their tendency toward mistakes, you also learn to love yourself. Self-acceptance and self-expression enable you to forgive yourself for violating your cardinal principles as you recalibrate and strive for greater integrity. Being true to yourself in turn best prepares you for your choice of friends and acquaintances. Genuine friends are made when you unconditionally accept yourself, because your friends do not attempt to manipulate you or tell you who you are. They wish to share your life's journey because they admire your ability to accept and express yourself without the need for external affirmation. Additionally, self-acceptance teaches you how to love God and other people as you love yourself. Self-acceptance is not a synonym for egotism or self-aggrandizement. It is an emotionally, psychologically and spiritually healthy way of living and relating to a power greater than you, esteeming yourself in proper proportion and considering the well-being and rights of other people. Self-acceptance further empowers you to define and develop your unique mission and purpose. In essence, self-acceptance means rightly relating to Almighty God, who lovingly esteems you as a unique child of His and encourages you to accept your divine character and distinction as you respectfully relate to each of your brothers and sisters in the human family. Grasping that simple yet significant concept heals and resurrects you from any rejection you experience.

"Forgiveness opens your eyes to the cares of the people you love around you even when you don't realize how much you love those who are around you."

As you listen to my story and share my experiences, I hope that you will embrace the process of healing and find encouragement and empowerment to seek renewal in your personal life and development. Focus upon the process of healing and not the product. Healing is a choice. Denial will not save you. Assuredly, it further holds you hostage, as opposed to liberating you. Each day, denial of your need for healing sieves more and more life, creativity, joy, happiness and peace of mind out of your mind, heart and soul. It kills you existentially before your physical expiration. Refusing to address my rejection complex and identity crisis would have made me a victim for the rest of my life. I would have lived with the daily and prevalent excuse, "I am like this because I was abandoned by my parents at birth." That line would become my get out of jail free card.

Repeatedly, I would recite it to evade responsibility and accountability in all areas of my life. I hope you will not remain stuck in the quicksand of rejection. The people who experience resurrection choose it through their faithfulness and resilience in the healing process. Healing is a gift for those persons who want it, and not the people who necessarily need it. Hence, healing necessitates perseverance and commitment. It requires steadfast practice of spiritual disciplines. Healing may impose counseling and other forms of supplemental treatment inclusive of residential treatment and twelve-step programs. Healing primarily and permanently occurs within relationships and communities. Healing is a gift of Almighty God.

Parenthetically, I am unabashedly and unapologetically a Christian. From a confessional perspective, I invite you to consider the truth of the Gospel of John the evangelist as he posits throughout his gospel that an encounter with Jesus Christ results in a wholesale transformation of a person's life. Spanning Nicodemus' nighttime conversation, to a Samaritan woman at a desert well, to a lame man for thirty-eight years beside a pool, to Lazarus' resurrection from his interment in a graveyard in Bethany, the evangelist asserts that anyone whose life intersects with Jesus Christ receives the gift of eternal life and discovers an eternal purpose to fulfill in this life. Practically speaking, Jesus instantaneously resurrects persons who linger in existential death. Hence, the evangelist offers that anyone who hears the words of Christ and believes He is the Son of God crosses over from death into eternal life. I hasten to add that this encounter begins a lifelong and eternal relationship. It is not a religious ritual. As with any vibrant relationship, it requires faithful commitment. Further, as a twenty-first century American citizen, who appreciates pluralism, diversity and globalization, I respect myriad expressions of genuine and intellectually respectable spirituality. I still, however, steadfastly suggest and prefer a Christian perspective, which I experientially and theoretically know yields inner healing and wholeness to anyone.

YOU CAN LOVE AND BE LOVED

One of the greatest joys in my healing process is learning to love with passion, faithfulness, intensity and happiness. When I love, I love fiercely with height, depth, breadth and width. When people overcome their fears relating to love, they generally love with strength and devotion exceeding the average person. Interestingly, fear hides the passion and commitment of many loving people who appear hard and exacting externally, but internally are very compassionate and understanding people, who will defend ferociously the people whom they love and bear any burden to demonstrate their loyalty and love. Fear of rejection impedes their willingness to begin a love relationship. Additionally, fear creates unrealistic expectations of loved ones and significant others. After all, we human beings love other equally fallible and imperfect human beings who will disappoint and fail us. To avoid rejection and pain, wounded persons attempt to dictate the terms and manner in which others love us. We only receive their affection as authentic if it unfolds in our love language. Ironically, we reject their love if it emerges in any way other than what we expect. Rather than humbly accepting their love as genuine, we wrongly conclude that they, too, are rejecting us because they fail to love us as we explicitly desire. In time, this mental dilemma and emotional agony eventuates in a self-fulfilling prophecy; we experience the rejection of another failed relationship as our impracticable expectations and unreasonable demands demean and demoralize loved ones, significant others and friends. They simply stop trying as their love proves inadequate for us. Consider the power of deep-seated and unresolved wounds to undermine any relationship. You are responsible for healing your own wounds, regardless of how deep they are and how long you've had them. Another person cannot cure you no matter how patient and loving they may be. The healing you seek is a gift of Almighty God who gives freely to anyone who humbly and sincerely asks.

DON'T TAKE YOUR LIFE FOR GRANTED

I conclude this preface with a word of encouragement and empowerment. God daily resurrects people to new life! My story is not unique. Though very difficult and painful as the forthcoming pages will reveal, my journey culminates in continued healing and hope. I unequivocally offer personal assurance of healing and hope to anyone who embraces the process of transcending rejection. I regret any hardships and suffering you experienced. Specifically, I am sorry for any scars of unrequited love, whether from a romantic interest or your family. I wish other people had the capacity and willingness to see you for who you are and appropriately honor, respect and accept you. I am very sorry they ignorantly and indifferently rejected you. However, I truly hope your investment of time and commitment in reading this book will yield willingness and power for your own healing process. Allow me to just recap some reasons why I am thankful for my parents. Likewise, you can find healing if you learn how to think about the things and people you are thankful for.

I am thankful to my parents for several reasons, and here are some.

- *They adopted me and loved me when everyone else walked by and passed me up because I was a sickly child.*

- *My father loved on my mother. I used to always think it was ugly to see them kissing one another, but now that I am married, I have learned the value of expressing love because I saw it growing up.*

- *They nurtured me in a Christian home and gave me unconditional love.*

- *They taught me the value of respecting others and myself.*

- *They took time to listen to me and give me things that money could never buy.*

- *They made sacrifices for me that I was unaware of, like taking out loans and almost having the check garnished just to keep me in college.*

- *My father always told me, "Son, if you are not better than I am in life, I did not do my job."*

- *They taught me to trust God at an early age.*

- *They showed me the importance of being generous towards others…my parents always gave their last.*

- *They supported me in all of my decisions in life, even ones that they thought were crazy.*

- *My father was and is the model of how a father and a husband should be.*

- *My mother taught me how to be kind to people. When she saw people in need, she would give money freely without expecting it to be returned.*

- *My mother would fight for me…she came outside with a knife one day because she heard someone was messing with her child. Keep in mind, she was a deaconess in our church, but when it came to her child, like any mother, she would do anything to protect them.*

- *They made sure they knew my whereabouts at all times. I appreciate it now because it showed me that they didn't just want me hanging out with anyone anywhere.*

- *They had the adoption papers for me and gave them to me. They said that they knew the day would come when I would ask for them. That really showed me that they were not trying to avoid it, but they were already prepared for that day.*

- *They whipped my behind when I was bad. I did not get a lot of whippings in life, but I did get enough to keep me on the straight and narrow. I always tell people, I feared my father long before I feared my Lord. And I am thankful for that. Too many youth of today do not have a healthy respect of their parents. And I believe if they do not respect their parents, there is no way they will respect others.*

- *They always made their home available to others. Although I am the only child, I never really lived alone. My parents always turned our home into the Carter Extended Stay Hotel. I used to resent it, but I have grown to appreciate and respect their decisions.*

- *So many other things I can say…*

ENDNOTES

1   Donne, John. No Man is An Island originally published in1624 in Devotions upon Emergent Occasions http://www.poemhunter.com/poem/no-man-is-an-island

2   Jung, Carl Gustav.   The Archetypes and the Collective Unconscious (R. F. C. Hull, translator, Princeton University Press: Princeton, NJ, 1969, pp.123 and 262).

HEALING 1
YOU ARE SOMEBODY: HEALING FROM REJECTION OF SELF

"The worst loneliness is to not be comfortable with yourself." –Mark Twain [1]

THE TRUTH CAN BE HURTFUL

"Steven, it's true, you are adopted but we love you like you are our own." Said with genuine and loving humility and an earnest desire to eliminate, miraculously and instantly, any pain her admission caused, my mother's words confirmed my worst fears. On the morning following my aunt's verbal smart-bomb informing me of my adoption, my parents and I gathered to process her hurtful, indifferent and happenstance revelation. Exaggeration rarely convinces anyone, yet I vividly recall feeling as if I had been hit with a sledgehammer. "Wow, all of this time, my cousins who have been hinting about my adoption have been telling the truth. I am an adopted child." Throughout this conversation, my parents repeatedly asked me if I were alright. Naturally, I said that I was fine, but I silently determined if they could mislead me for thirteen years, I too would lie until I felt like sharing my true and raw emotions. I would wait for the moment when someone would tell them, "Steven has been hurting for a long time since the two of you waited for someone else to tell him that he is not your biological child." Their words and my thoughts combined as I began the journey of searching for my essential identity. Rather than clarifying an abrupt but severe miscommunication, my parents *matter-of-fact* confirmation of my adoption equated with an internment of my

mind, heart, emotions and soul for the next twenty-three years. I died emotionally. Their words evaporated into thin air. I descended into a grave of rejection.

That chance conversation I had with my parents is the real defining moment of my life. Their gracious acknowledgement of my aunt's slip of the mouth and earnest wishes to eradicate my pain could not eliminate the identity crisis that I had. My concept of myself as their son had been decimated with their admission. I was left with the primary question, "Who am I?" My previous answer to that question no longer sufficed. Really, I wanted to know who I had been as I was misguided to believe I was an equal and accepted member of my family. "From this day, who am I? Will I succumb to the temptation of acting as if I had not heard my aunt?" Living through the trauma of rejection and loss of identity, I spent the balance of my adolescence and early adult years seeking reliable answers to these questions.

Subsequent to the talk with my parents, I learned that I had been a sickly, premature baby at birth. Seeking to adopt a child, my parents still choose to proceed though circumstance, and fate had given them a less than perfect child. With great pain, I also later learned that my paternal grandmother advised my father against adopting me. On her death bed, she confessed to me that her mother's heart sought to protect my father from the future pain of my death as an infant. Before I was six months old, I had had five operations. Among my physical challenges were a hole in my heart, a hernia and a twisted intestine. I was and am a personified miracle. Still, my physical infirmities presented my biological parents with a dilemma. For reasons known forever only to them, they chose to put me up for adoption. I presume the challenge of rearing a child with my birth defects seemed insurmountable to them. Possibly, the expense of my operations and long-term care presented a financial crisis they could not bear. In addition, there was always the chance that I would not survive despite their emotional, monetary and parental commitment They may have thought it was best and easiest to place me up for adoption. Perhaps, they would forego the potential disappointment and heartache of attempting to save a child who was going to die regardless of their valiant efforts. Again, I can only speculate as I have never heard their perspective or had the privilege of admission to the inner chambers of their hearts to listen to their raw feelings and honest thoughts. I will not know how long or hard they debated their decision. I would like to believe it was the most difficult choice they have ever made. Given its impact upon my life, I hope my biological parents revisited their decision with fervent prayer about its correctness. Have they ever second-guessed themselves? Did they remember to pray and ask God to bless their decision? Have they ever wished that they could share in my life? I will not ask any more of these questions as it is painful, still, to do so and I will never know the answers. However, I do know that whatever their thoughts and feelings at the time, my biological parents seemingly had no idea that I would receive their decision as a categorical rejection of me and my personhood.

Parenthetically, I am unaware of my biological parents' challenges. I do not know if they experienced any. I am aware that they had five other children, and I was number six, and my mother was allegedly not even at the tender age of 30. Were I to extend to them the benefit of the doubt, I conjecture my anticipated terminal illness greatly surpassed their abilities as parents. Realizing their severe limitations helped them to decide upon adoption. My siblings were probably told that I was a still born infant who is now in heaven. Family hearsay informs me that my biological parents chose not to see me at birth. As a consequence, I partially reason that their decision was not a hard one. However, I can equally extrapolate that the difficulty, severity and permanence of the decision is also why they elected not to see me. Perhaps, they did not want the image of their innocent and helpless child wiggling, thereby appealing to their natural instinct and parental heart, to form indelibly in their minds. I imagine such an image would haunt them for the rest of their lives and prevent them from ever experiencing any semblance of peace of mind. As my suppositions will remain forever unanswered in this life, I will release them as I have forgiven my biological parents and released them from my expectations and judgment of what they should have done.

> ### "Forgiveness is never for the individual being forgiven; forgiveness is always to free yourself from the self-imposed bondage of being unforgiving towards another person."

Their choice to alleviate themselves of the burden of me in turn became a millstone I would carry during the first half of my life. My adoptive parents' decision to withhold this vital information compounded my agony and grief. However well-intentioned all of them were, their choices resulted in a victim's complex and a self-esteem crisis in which I viewed myself as the slightly, but permanently, damaged toy on the clearance table in the dollar store. Perhaps, a kid who happened to have the right amount of change in his pockets would decide to purchase me, take me home and play with me, until he could afford a brand new toy of course. My parents' revelation on the morning of that fateful conversation felt similarly. In my mind, I went from being their beloved son to seeing myself as a goodwill project. I no longer felt as if I had the actual rights, immunities, privileges and blessings of a "real" son. In fact, my aunt had told me as much in her instructions that I attend immediately to any directives I receive in gratitude for my parents' largesse of heart and longstanding charity. In response to the abundant rejection I felt at the hands of my biological parents and patronizing kindness of my adoptive parents, I began to reject myself.

WHEN REJECTION MOTIVATES YOUR SUCCESSES

What I discovered was that my parents did not reject ME, they rejected the responsibility that came with keeping me. However, I did not know this fact until recently as I began this book process. Therefore, in my young years, instead of turning to alcohol, drugs, illicit sex and other addictive escapes, I developed assertive and defensive qualities in my character. The blissful naiveté of my previous thirteen years ended summarily and immediately. Everything I believed about love, family and myself had been shattered. Realizing that I was adopted was the antithesis of everything I thought about my parents, family and me. Now, I had the grueling and unpredictable task of picking up the shards of what I thought was the sacred, stained glass mosaic of my wonderful life. How would I put these many pieces, what had been smashed to smithereens, back together into a holistic and beautiful montage? First, Paul Ricoeur, the philosopher and possible theologian, posits that each person progresses from his first naiveté to a second one that he holds securely for the balance of his life.[2] As many churchgoing Christians and local pastors are prone to beautiful pronouncements of faith, I simply could have asserted the blessing of being adopted and beautified my adoptive parents thereby suppressing the punishing and harsh emotions their revelation caused me. I am sure my aunt, extended family members and friends would have applauded this approach of denying my pain and forcing myself to wear a mask of ecstatic gratitude. Secondly, Hegel offers his immortal triad of personal maturity: being, non-being and becoming; some persons characterize Hegel's system as thesis, antithesis and synthesis.[3] My adoptive parents' confirmation of my aunt's words catapulted me to the second stage of Hegel's system. I was living with the antithesis of every emotion and feeling that my heart held dear. Putting the shards of your life back together does not parallel completing a thousand-pieces or more jigsaw puzzle as you have a perfect picture that the puzzle makes. Smashed pieces of stain glass do not fit together as neatly or quickly. Shattered truths in a person's life also are not easily dismissed or replaced. Yet, I had no choice but to progress toward some type of synthesis for my life that enabled me to love without bitterness and trust, avoiding cynicism. Thirdly, Carl Gustav Jung describes the formation and concretization of the "Shadow" in a person's character. This dark side of the persona solidifies as patterns of thought in consciousness, behavior and temperament that create resistance to a person's good and growth. Practically speaking, the "Shadow" compels a person toward delusions and self-sabotage. He blames his inability to cultivate meaningful relationships upon everyone else. His long and wide shadow obscures the ways in which he immediately undermines any possibility of mutually beneficial and respectful relationships with anyone. Under the guise of having integrity and being forthright, he defensively offends persons he just met who distance themselves from him as they suspect he will become a future adversary. As a new adolescent without any knowledge or psychology or any training in spiritual disciplines such as self-evaluation and meditation, I chose to foster a huge shadow to protect myself from any possibility of any future pain.

HURT PEOPLE HURT PEOPLE

My anger would fuel my defensiveness, assertiveness and victim's complex for the next twenty-two years. In simple words, I developed a constant ongoing chip on my shoulder. I would fight and scrape for my self-worth and well-being. I could no longer trust the people near me to do so. I felt as if they had lied to me for thirteen years. I would make anyone and everyone in the world wake up and notice Steven Eugene Carter! My righteous indignation made me assertive. I would not take "NO" from anyone. Regardless of the issue and however small or large, I had to have my way. I became impatient with people. I had to have what I wanted when I desired it. I blamed my assertive and defensiveness on my biological parents. They made me this way because they rejected me. Someone had to correct their mistake. I could no longer rely upon my adoptive parents to do so as they had united with the rest of the family to hide my dreadful secret. With each fleeting thought about any of this complex and bewildering burden of emotions and relationships, I became incensed. I took offense when and where none was meant. I doggedly and forthrightly clarified any miscommunication usually informing the other person just how wrong they were. In a crowd of people, I made sure that I stood out. I would not be average again. Initially, my alma mater, *Morehouse College*, rejected my application for admission. In response, I enrolled at a neighboring school but in the summer after my first year of college, I returned to the admission office and boldly declared their mistake. After matriculating to Morehouse, whose student body comprises collegiate men of impressive and considerable ability, aptitude and achievement, I made sure that everyone understood that I had superlative potential amongst such an august student body. Defensively, I thought of myself as the *crème de la crème* of the *crème de la crème*. An egomaniac with an inferiority complex, I resolved to bury my rejection with arrogance, defensiveness and excessive compensation and achievement.

"Hurt people, hurt people. So if you find yourself always hurting people, maybe you have some hurts in your life that you have not recovered from."

Hidden beneath the external bravado and loquacious justification for my existence and esteem was my raw pain and lingering hurt that the persons who partnered to conceive me did not care or love me enough to rear me. As is usually the case, my anger cloaked my victim's complex and entrenched limiting beliefs about my self-worth and self-image. How could I feel good about myself if my very own parents did not love me enough to care for me? What was my worth if they did not assign any value to me? Given that my adoption was a longstanding family secret, what alternative did my family have other than to view me as a charity case? My defensive anger enflamed these destructive beliefs within my mind and heart instead of incinerating them. My ferocious anger demonstrated that I actually uncritically *accepted* other people's estimation and opinions of me.

Rejected persons live with perpetual anger which hopefully decreases consistently and gradually as they heal. Its intensity is inescapable. Anger flavors anything rejected people say or do. I have had a very short temper. After learning that I was adopted, I was nearly expelled from my high school (Washington Irving in Manhattan, New York) because of a proliferation of fights with my teachers. I was headed to the High School of Redirection. As a result of trying to help me improve, I was transferred to Thomas Jefferson High School of Brooklyn, New York; which was the zone school for where my family resided. Years later, I served on the ministerial staff of Brentwood Baptist Church in Houston, Texas. I threatened my supervisor who greatly upset me with an off hand remark that I found offensive. Believing he was attempting to humiliate me, my anger rose to rage and I said, "I will put a cap in your ass negro." Retrospectively, I am glad he looked beyond my character defect and improbable murderous threat; he was much taller and bigger than I am. While living in Houston, I had a license to carry a gun. On a random day, a guy cut me off in traffic. Immediately, I took offense and yelled at him. When we stopped at the next red light, he got out of his car and approached my window. After rolling down the window and pointing a Glock .23 caliber pistol at him, I asked, "Would you like to carry this any further?" He quickly retreated and returned to his vehicle. Later that day, despite the raging forest fire of emotions in my mind and heart because of my rejection and anger, I had the common sense to sell that weapon. I realized my anger would eventually result in my incarceration or physical death.

Additionally, in my later years, my anger made me hurt people whom I serve, like and love as a pastor. My unresolved anger, stemming from my abandonment and betrayal, consumed anything I experienced and any relationship, professional or personal, that I cultivated. Like an uncontained forest fire, my deep-seated anger about being adopted heretofore burned and devastated the emotions and feelings of anyone in its path. I shudder to think about the countless persons I have hurt because of my pain. I have terminated people. I have been condescending to people. I have belittled and demeaned people. Regularly when questioned about any decisions, I issued ultimatums. "It will be my way or the highway!" In my early thirties, I was still living in my adolescent anger. Genuinely, I wish I could retrieve and nullify thousands of unwise, poisonous and painful words I uttered to undeserving, kind and well-intentioned people. As I accept the hard reality that I cannot, I further commit to healing from my pain. My experience of abandonment and adoption is not a license to hurt other people. I cannot utilize it to evade responsibility for my choices and behavior as an adult. Just as I rightly relinquished the gun that would have contributed to my physical death, I forever renounce my rejection and victim's complex which would seal my existential death.

The dissolution of my anger, which had petrified within my mind and heart over the twenty-two years between my thirteenth and thirty-fifth birthdays, is the story of my resurrection from rejection. I have experienced every range of anger, venom, bitterness, strife, vexation and vengeance possible. I wanted everyone to feel the pain and disappointment I feel. I felt justified in my anger and rage; after all, even animals in the wild do not needlessly abandon their children. Against much larger predators and foes, they fight for the survival of their offspring. Why would my biological parents not face the adversities of extreme sickness of their son and formidable financial challenges to fight for my survival? Why couldn't my adoptive parents have honored their choice and my dignity by disclosing their loving and compassionate choice to adopt me in an equally loving and considerate way? My responses to people regarding simple and insignificant questions were laced with venom. If I offered criticisms of anyone, I did so in the most destructive way. Again, I belittled, demeaned and dehumanized people to the same extent that I felt these emotions. I nursed the bitterness and bewilderment I felt. I found myself in constant conflict with practically everyone. Each day, I rose to rejoin the battles of the previous day. Though I perfected a public persona to the contrary of liking everyone and granting people the benefit of the doubt, I trusted absolutely no one. Sometimes I even asked myself if I could trust God.

However, that thought quickly faded as I knew I could. I felt like the man in Scripture who said, "Lord I believe, just help my unbelief," (Mark 9:24, NIV). I reasoned that my adoptive parents' betrayal meant that I could not depend upon any other human being for my emotional well-being and psychological security. My progress toward resurrection necessitated my acquisition of genuine reliance upon Almighty God to heal my pain and hurt. Heretofore, I lived a self-reliant life forsaking the necessity of an interdependent relationship with a power greater than me. Nonetheless, I was angry with God for letting the adoption happen and I was angry with everyone else because it occurred and forever changed the way I would view myself. Instead of asking God to show His will to me and depending upon Him to maneuver the situations of my life toward my ultimate good, I focused significantly upon my pain. Because my distress was so severe, I wanted other people to feel discomfort and grief in the same proportions as I felt. Particularly, I thought it fair and just that my biological parents receive due punishment for the irreparable injury they inflicted upon me. I wanted them to know how it feels to second guess your very existence practically every minute of the day. I wanted them to cry until their tear ducts dried up. I wanted them to face heartache and humiliation. I wanted them to pay for their crimes! At one point in my childhood, I planned to enter law enforcement. I now grasp that that ambition evolved from my resentment that my biological parents were fugitives who escaped any accountability for their bastardly deeds. As it relates to my adoptive parents, I personally would ensure they paid retribution for their deceit and duplicity. I made the decision that as soon as I was old enough to leave their caring home, I would leave and never again request any help from them, which I knew would ache them badly because they are two individuals who pride themselves on helping so many people, which I witnessed growing up as a child in such a caring home. Therefore,

I knew that if I robbed them of the opportunity to continue to care for their son, the pain it would cause them would serve as some payments for the pain that I felt they caused me by keeping my reality hidden from me. The foregoing characterizations and reflections upon my anger and other emotions during my twenty-two years of entombment to rejection are hardly exhaustive. Yet, I trust they suffice to vividly depict how far I descended into rejection of myself in response to my perceived rejection of my parents, family and other people.

"Sometimes God will allow you to have low moments in your life, not for the purpose of keeping you down, but so you can find other people who may be low and lift them out of their self-imposed caves as a result of your own resurrection."

Prior to marriage, I did not accept critical insight from anyone unless they possessed some type of influence or control in my life. Other than my parents, the only persons who I allowed to have significant influence over me were Dr. and Mrs. Elliott Cuff, Dr. Joe Samuel Ratliff and Dr. Ralph Douglas West. In my mind, any other person was someone who would one day disappoint me, and I chose to never give anyone that chance. I always demanded the truth up front. As the truth was hidden from me for thirteen years, I would no longer tolerate delayed truth from anyone. My intuition senses hesitation and immediately coerces me to push for straightforward answers to my questions. I resent any efforts to massage my feelings or prevent me from feeling pain. Lying is very hurtful and insulting. I learned to dismiss people who withheld vital truths from me. I could not accept anything as genuine from such persons. I know people proactively withhold information in order to "keep the peace." However, I do not agree with any concept of peace that utilizes false and questionable means to accomplish immoral and unethical objectives. Deceiving children in their formative years quite possibly eradicates their ability to open their minds and hearts to people. Parents risk obliterating their children's future emotional and psychological security, which is necessary to healthy and trustworthy relationships. My healing process continues to grace me with increasing willingness and ability to trust other people who demonstrate integrity.

I ask you to journey with me as a fellow traveler in a process of healing, which is the main motif of retelling my story in this book. I am not a pathologist. Accordingly, I have not invited you to observe an autopsy. Instead, I ask you to think, ponder and meditate on your own need, process and journey toward healing. Try to identify with my thoughts and feelings; resist the impulse to contrast our stories. Rejection is rejection regardless of its type. Though each individual deals differently with trauma and adversity, the range of feelings is common in the human experience. I hope you continually and mystically receive encouragement and empowerment as you share my journey.

QUESTIONS TO ASK YOURSELF

Do you struggle with self-acceptance? Has your life been one identity crisis after another? Have you experienced a colossal rejection of your personhood? Are you constantly seeking validation from other people? Do you live vicariously through someone else? Are you drawn to emulating another person's life? Do you insult and criticize other people in order to feel good about yourself? Do you struggle with any addictions such as alcohol, drugs, sex, eating, gambling and debt? Does satiating your physical instincts and satisfying your emotional impulses command considerable amounts of your time and energy? Are you easily offended? Are you hypersensitive to any type of criticism? Must you always have the last word? Do you always have to be right? Is being right more important than being in right relationship with people? Have you retained childhood, limiting beliefs about your character, physical appearance, abilities and talents? Do you constantly feel as if you have something to prove? Your answers to these questions are potential indicators of an identity crisis. Multiple affirmative replies to those questions mean we share the burden of recovering and healing from rejection. This process is glacial. There is no magic wand to wave and eliminate decades of compounded pain. One day at a time, when you commit to healing, you will receive God's grace, love and peace of mind. Healing demands faithfulness and fortitude. The process lasts longer than reading this book, though it is a first step of sorts in your journey toward wellness, healing and wholeness.

"You will never be able to fix what you are first unwilling to face. Ask God to give you the strength to face issues in your life that need fixing."

Healing in its simplest and surest form magnifies in your mind, heart and soul as you acquire increasing self-acceptance. Persons who unconditionally accept, approve, love and express their individuality and esteem their unique personalities as God does have been resurrected from rejection. They annihilate their anger. Their hearts contain passion, purpose and love. Instead of being an active volcano from which people recoil, they personify divine light, love, grace, mercy, humility and peace.

Persons in the healing process renounce their victim's complex and surrender their use of abandonment as a blanket excuse for their behavior and choices. As the "masters of our minds," we control our choices, thoughts, emotions and actions. We forfeit the license to hurt other people because we have been injured. We learn the practical and pragmatic means of redirecting our frustrations and pain toward redemptive and empowering purposes. We cease making excuses and embrace life on its terms. As a Christian, I understand the ghastly deed of Christ's crucifixion as the ideal experience of redemption suffering in human history. Good Friday means crucifixion always yields resurrection. God raises Jesus from the dead on the first Easter morning thereby transforming His pain and suffering into new life. In the process of healing to wholeness from rejection, similarly you experience resurrection from your rejection pains.

Unresolved feelings and lingering miscommunication poison relationships and retard healing. I had to learn to forgive my biological parents as my anger and other fierce emotions coalesced around them. Forgiveness means to pardon; you forego your right to retributive justice and punishment. When you forgive, you act as if the original offense and harm never occurred parallel to a governor's pardon of a criminal whose crime is expunged from legal records upon his release from imprisonment. Ironically, as I pardoned my biological parents, I actually liberated myself from my entombment of rejection. I now increasingly receive and live within happiness, joy and freedom. I do not know if they ever felt they needed my forgiveness. I do not know if they ever suffered with their decision. Did they experience sleepless nights wondering whether they made the right decision? On any winter night, were they concerned about whether I had adequate clothing for the season as I traveled to and from school? The answers no longer matter as I wholeheartedly have forgiven them. In the starkest irony of all, I appreciate my biological parents and their choice to put me up for adoption. Their action enabled my adoption by my beloved parents and my membership in an equally loving family who nurtured and empowered me to discover my uniqueness as a child of God. Transforming anger into gratitude is the means of acquiring forgiveness and freedom.

Visualization is a timely method of curing illnesses and resolving personal problems. Several prominent secular spiritual teachers recommend its consistent practice as a means of surmounting adversities. In fact, Hebrews 11:1 lends itself to a translation that equates faith with visualization: "Faith is the substance of things hoped for and the evidence of things not seen." Through the eyes of your heart, you see the things you want until they manifest empirically. As you journey toward healing from rejection and expect resurrection, you envision the day when you will stand before a full length mirror and unconditionally accept, approve, love and express the person whom you see. After the revelation and confirmation of my adoption and the intensity of my anger subsided, I created fantasies of a great and wonderful life. I imagined meeting one of my siblings who possibly played in the NBA or NFL. Upon his hearing of my unfortunate story and sympathizing for me as his wounded brother who was categorically unlucky, he would share his wealth with me. I would not have to work again. Also, I envisioned meeting my biological parents and establishing a loving and longstanding relationship with them as if the adoption had not happened. Not knowing my genealogical origins, I even recently daydreamed about the possibility of being related to President Barack Obama, the first African American President of the United States. After falling through the clouds and landing back in the Earth's atmosphere, I began to wonder whether I was related to Oprah

Winfrey, who would not be a bad auntie to have. Whereas my fantasies were so impractical and improbable, visualization, supplemented with prayer and meditation, greatly aided me in transcending my emotional and experiential hardships. This spiritual discipline opens the windows of my soul to a fourth dimension of existence that transcends life's daily limitations and enables me to actualize my spiritual and eternal essence.

"Dream big dreams, and if that doesn't work, dream BIGGER dreams."

I hope you experience a personal and enduring resurrection from rejection. I hope you are able to cease the harmful and dreadful practice of rejecting yourself because other people initially denied you. I conclude this chapter with a few helpful healing suggestions to build and strengthen self-acceptance.

"Wanting to be someone else is a waste of who you are."—Kurt Cobain[4]

12 THINGS TO UNDERSTAND ABOUT YOURSELF

1. You were not born by accident. God created you and gave you a unique life that only you can receive and live. Ultimately, your birth did not emerge from human intention and biology. God made you in His image to share His love in a unique way with humankind.

2. You have a unique, individual and specific purpose that only you can fulfill.

3. You are "fearfully and wonderfully made" in the image of Almighty God. Read Psalm 139 each day for a month.

4. You can live the life you imagine, despite your past pain and personal history.

5. You can be comfortable in your skin as you accept, approve, love and express yourself.

6. Learn to live and let live.

7. There is no need to compete with anyone.

8. Learn how to detect the emergence of your self-sabotaging behavioral patterns. Release your need for them. You are fine as you are. Other people will know this truth and learn to appreciate you.

9. Learn how to recognize, discard, neutralize and eliminate patterns of consciousness that create resistance to your good and adverse patterns of character that impede your growth.

10. Learn how to redirect your thoughts, words and behavior.

11. Gain validation through unpaid service as a volunteer in your local community assisting senior citizens, homeless persons and families, needy at-risk youth or some other vulnerable residents. As you encourage and empower other people with direct service and hope, you actually help yourself. You learn to be grateful and to accept yourself as a caring, giving and compassionate person.

12. You have the right to live in unconditional self-acceptance and with peace of mind and heart.

REVIEW QUESTIONS

What truths in your life do you not like admitting? (Be honest with yourself)

_____

_____

_____

Who are some people in your life you know you need to forgive? Write their names down and pray and ask God to give you a forgiving spirit. Remember, forgiveness is for you and not the person.

_____

_____

_____

What are some painful experiences in your life that have made you a better person?

_____

_____

_____

In what ways do you hurt people because of the hurts you carry in your life? Write it down and submit it to the Lord to deliver you from it.

_____

_____

_____

What in your life specifically made/makes you feel rejected?

_____

_____

_____

What are three things you will do to help you move towards your healing?

I will _____

I will _____

I will _____

Please write down the REAL reason you purchased this book. When you feel like quitting, refer back to the reason you purchased this book. *I purchased this book because....*

_____

_____

_____

ENDNOTES

1   Mark Twain (Samuel Langhorne Clemens) http://www.
goodreads.com/quotes/83918-the-worst-loneliness-is-to-not-be-
comfortable-with-yourself

2   Ricoeur, Paul. *The Symbolism of Evil* (Boston: Beacon Press,
1967)

3   Hegel, George Wilhelm Friedrich. *The Science of Logic*
(Cambridge University Press, 2010 edition)

4   http://www.brainyquote.com/quotes/quotes/k/
kurtcobain183004.html

HEALING 2
YOU ARE FAMILY: HEALING FROM REJECTION FROM RELATIVES

"You don't choose your family, they are chosen by God." —Desmond Tutu[1]

WHEN HURT COMES FROM INSIDE THE FAMILY

It is commonly said that blood is thicker than water. My experience as an adopted son teaches me otherwise. Sometimes, blood is much thinner than water. The indifference of biological parents defies characterization and explanation. Conversely, the authentic and divine love of adoptive parents exceeds anyone's expectations. Like the selfless, sacrificial, redemptive and transformative love of Jesus Christ which St. John the evangelist details in his Gospels and Epistles, the genuine love of adoptive parents possibly surpasses the obligatory, socially conventional, traditional and dutiful love of biological parents. My journey teaches me that love begins and is appreciated within mutually respectful relationships, whether parent and child, husband and wife, cousins in an extended family or best friends. When human beings experientially and relationally grasp and emulate divine love, particularly God's love as revealed in the Person and teachings of Jesus Christ, they transcend historical and contemporary conceptualizations of love's affects and effects. I increasingly appreciate the myriad of mystical and mysterious ways in which genuine love, shared between people who have no biological connection, legacy or heritage, can exceed human expectations and delimitations of love.

Though we consider the nuclear family unit to be the primary unit of love, nurture, training, encouragement and empowerment, it is also the most destructive environment for many people. How often have we heard talk show guests explain their character defects, crimes and deviant behavior as results of having grown up in a dysfunctional family. Hidden beneath the gloss of social respectability is the emotional and experiential trauma of incest, molestation, infidelity, unemployment, poverty, mental illness, hypocrisy and other types of toxic behaviors that denigrate and demean anyone in the family. Parents who suffer with grave emotional challenges hardly qualify to instruct their children about upright moral and ethical principles. Instead, their dysfunctional behaviors become the yardstick with which their children measure their progress toward maturity and adulthood. Children observing grown men and women drinking, swearing, smoking and having illicit sex believe those behaviors indicate a person's arrival into their adult years.

Further, American citizens may demythologize the television and screen images of perfect families projected into households since the 1950s. The Cleaver family of *Leave It to Beaver* and the ideal loving, patient and understanding father played by Fred MacMurray in *My Three Sons* are fictional characters created by cultural elite writers, directors and producers seeking to determine the moral fiber of the nation. Reportedly, MacMurray hardly spoke with any of his fellow cast members or stage crew off camera. He insisted that his scenes be done first so that he could leave. Additional shows such as *Father Knows Best*, *The Brady Bunch* and *The Cosby Show* expanded the enduring myth of the perfect family with ideally loving parents and siblings, despite life's daily complexities. Allegedly, Robert Young was a raving alcoholic whose personal and private life suffered tremendously during the entire run of the show. In

"Where are They Now" interviews, cast members of *The Brady Bunch* share their very deep regret for contributing to the farce of America's ideal adopted and blended family. The actor who played Michael Brady, Mike Lookinland, reminds everyone that everything about television is not real. Situated in the complexities and shifting social mores of the late 1980s and early 1990s, *The Cosby Show* still fostered gilded images of a middle-class, bourgeois, blended and extended African American family. In daily living within the Earth's gravitational pull, the quest for self-acceptance is a very individual, personal, and perhaps lonely process. A person's family may contribute favorably in assisting and empowering him to find and develop his true self. Most regrettably, his family may also be the biggest hindrance he encounters as he embarks upon the journey to wellness, healing, identity, and wholeness.

"The LOVE of a family is life's greatest blessings." —Author unknown

MY FAMILY

My family of origin consisted of my adoptive father, Deacon Eugene Carter, my adoptive mother, Deaconess Mary Carter, and me. Until the arrival of a foster brother, Shaun Alston, whom my parents added to our family to remove my potential isolation as an only child, I thoroughly enjoyed my solitude, serenity and surplus as the apple of my parents' eyes. My parents' leadership position in a local Baptist church, where I now serve as Senior Pastor, revealed the traditional religious upbringing I received. My parents' example as Christians and lay leaders laid the foundation of my calling and life as a pastor and clergyman. Beyond my collegiate experience and formal professional training in seminary, they modelled a genuine disciple's life. I expanded upon what I observed in them with my vocational choice when I was called by God into ministry at the age of 18.

However, my aunt's treacherous and enlightening words forever removed the veil of my blissful understanding of family. Prior to her admonition about taking out the trash, I existed in a womb of unbridled love, joy, happiness and peace. My aunt's words equated with eating from the tree of knowledge of good and evil. I would then struggle with love's layered complexity and perpetual ambiguity. Like humankind's infidelity that tainted the love our first human parents shared with God, my aunt's words opened my eyes to the nakedness of the scars, wounds and gashes that result from human love.

Notwithstanding their Christian example of love, my parents contributed to the loss of my innocence as they withheld the origins of our family. At thirteen years of age, I was unable to appreciate providence, agape love, redemption, forgiveness, and sovereignty. These formal theological terms I would study in my graduate training from a theoretical point of view. As I traversed the difficult terrain of emotions and experiences relating to receiving love via adoption, I gained an existential understanding of those terms. Now, I understand how Almighty God mystically sowed seeds of providence in my life through my adoptive parents. I know now that God's especial love, agape, is selfless, sacrificial and redemptive. This divine love, the most supreme type of love, transcends human categories, thereby enabling my adoptive parents to share genuinely divine love with me. They surmounted the social and conventional challenges that stipulate that only biological children are "real." Through faith in Christ and their understanding of God's adoption of all disciples in the family of God (Romans 11:11-24 and Galatians 4:4-7), they selflessly desired to share their love with an adoptive son by making the same sacrifices and empowering his character as they would have for a "biological" son. In His infinite wisdom, God orchestrates these details and composes families, thus placing children and parents in ideal matches to accomplish their individual and collective destinies. Parenthetically, a part of my personal destiny is the book you are reading; as my story of adoption, anger, rejection and healing hopefully encourages and empowers you in achieving your purpose and destiny.

Nonetheless, my adoptive parents' love redeemed the infidelity and rejection of my birth parents who lacked the capacity, commitment and faithfulness to fulfill their obligations. My parents' love and God's grace during the twenty-three years following my aunt's revelation motivated me to forgive my birth parents. Love is the basis of forgiveness as "love covers a multitude of sins," (1 Peter 4:8, NIV). Love enables a person to desire right relationship instead of right behavior. As an adoptive son, being in right relationship with my parents means more to me than demanding right action and retribution from my birth parents who abandoned and rejected me. Further, I forgive their incapacities, as they were unable to offer God's selfless, sacrificial and transformative love to me. As I write, I humbly and forthrightly acknowledge that God's plan for my upbringing through my adoptive parents' nurture and service was far better for me than what my birth parents would have done. In forgiving my birth parents, I extend God's love to them with a sincere hope that they love their five children as unconditionally as my adoptive parents love me.

GOD SENDS US WHO WE NEED

God's sovereign and unquestionable will ordered my life to enable me to be the son of Deacon and Deaconess Carter. I accept His mysterious and mystical blessing. God uses my parents to demonstrate His unfailing love to me. I no longer question His means and ways. My personal preferences are not important. Most definitely, God is not bound to historical and human conceptualizations of parenthood and nuclear families. Beyond the myriad theological texts I read in seminary, I know God's love as I experience its embodiment in my parents and extended family.

As loving as my parents and extended family were in my formative years, however, I still felt tremendous rejection from them. My aunt's words resembled the opening of Pandora's Box. I could not have known the different ways I would feel and receive rejection. Once she unearthed the dirty little secret of my adoption, it appeared that rejection occurred constantly. More often than I cared to hear, my father told me, "I love you as if you were my own biological child." Assuredly, he intended to reassure me of his love as a father for me as a son; adoption did not detract from the genuine love he holds in his heart. Each time he said those words, though, they became a dagger in my heart as they consistently reminded me that I was adopted. His love sufficed; a qualification or disclaimer about our type of relationship was unnecessary. Though I would not dare disrespect my father, I certainly wished he would have stopped saying those words…however well-intentioned they were. Second, cousins in my extended family were cruel. They would say many hurtful comments. "You are not blood." "Your parents get paid to keep you." "You were delivered by UPS." As a kid, I did not know how to respond. So, I internalized these damaging and destructive words. I began to feel as if I were living a lie as a member of my family. Feeling like an outsider in your family when you previously had emotional security is indescribable. Equally flabbergasting, their harsh words further isolated me as I struggled to comprehend the legitimacy of my family's love as an adopted outsider. My cousins would never know the extent of their verbal damage. To protect myself, I withdrew from them and retreated within me. I did not have the language of entombment at that tender age. Yet,

I knew how wrong it felt to be told that love exists between persons who share blood lines, legacy and lineage, but to receive seminal rejection from those people. Families of origin are not always the most supportive and affirming environments.

"You are not what people call you, you are only what you respond to."

The starkest and strangest episode of rejection within my family occurred when a female cousin made an incestuous request of me. She assured me that we could be sexual because we were not related biologically. She disregarded my relationship to her through our parents and extended family. Because we did not share the same gene pool, she relegated legitimate status as her cousin to being meaningless. The horror of incest and its many complications within a family did not matter to her. Her sexual overture disgusted me; actually, it causes my stomach to turn as I consider arrogance and hedonism embedded in her suggestion. Her empiricist outlook on human relationships belittled my moral principles and ethical understanding of family relationships, which I hold sacred and sacrosanct. Because of her ignorance of God's love through adoption, she devalued me and my personhood. She rejected my moral and ethical character only because we did not share biology.

In retrospect, I realize my grossly misguided cousin offered me a new perspective on family, in addition to one of my first fundamental moral and ethical quandaries. Her incestuous proposal gave me a chance to examine my definition of familial relationships. Beforehand, I castigated my birth parents for their rejection of me. I assumed that biology mandated that they reared me. Like some who naively depend upon the black letters of contracts, I thought traditional family values meant that they would be my primary caretakers and teachers because of our shared gene pool. I did not grasp the hard reality that relationships and commitment determine parenthood, not biology and genes. My cousin's proposal exposed my own myopia about family. Perhaps, her suggestion repulsed me because I unconsciously shared her clinical, scientific and empirical outlook upon family relationships. In the expanse of my twenty-three year odyssey from abandonment and rejection to resurrection, I learned to accept love as it emerges within respectful, emotionally healthy and ethical relationships between people. I find adoption as one of God's most effective means of ensuring His unique children receive the love, nurture and affirmation they need to discover their individuality and accomplish their destiny. Ironically, a vulgar and repulsive sexual advance from an ignorant cousin became a catalyst of enlightenment for me.

Lest I romanticize the foregoing instances of personal pain and familial rejection, I ask you to relinquish any lingering idealistic notions and expectations you have of your families of origin. In a perfect world, your nuclear and extended family would have been the perfect unit of instruction, encouragement, empowerment and love. Regrettably, it may have been the source of lifelong emotional and psychological challenges borne of agonizing and pervasive rejection. Sometimes, the people closest to us fail to see us and appreciate our distinct personalities. In addition, members of our family often assume they know us better than we know ourselves. Should we rebuff their attempts to define us, then we experience merciless humiliation and rejection. Whether concurring with any of my personal experiences of rejection by family members or harboring your very own, you can heal from this particularly debilitating type of rejection. As my cousin's incestuous opportunity helped me to redefine my understanding of family, you too will experience divergent plot twists in your healing process as you zigzag toward a happy, joyous and free life.

In an effort to protect myself, I responded to my family's rejection by withdrawing from them. When I say I withdrew from them, I mean it in every sense of the word. Years elapsed as I found convenient excuses to avoid family reunions that would take place in Littleton, North Carolina; the home city where my father was born and raised. I really did not feel as if I were a member of the family. To circumvent my feelings of shame, grief and loneliness when I was with my extended family, I created conflicts to cause my absence. My parents repeatedly bore embarrassment as I initially accepted invitations to preach at the Sunday worship service of these family reunions. In the week before the event, I would withdraw my acceptance. On a couple of occasions, I simply did not show up. My stinging and persistent feelings of rejection justified my rude and unnecessary behavior. In my heart, I nursed my resentments against my loved ones whom I felt rejected me. My isolation and absence became my means of reciprocating the pain.

THE DANGER OF ISOLATING YOURSELF

Looking back, if I could change the past, I would not have isolated myself from my family. I would more greatly value my relationships within my extended family. After detaching for so many years, it is hard to reconnect. Some family members were unwilling to invest sweat equity in rebuilding a distant relationship that they assumed had died. Inadvertently, I hurt people who merely sought to love me. Because of my preoccupation with my feelings of rejection and past pain I could not see that I in turn was hurting undeserving people. I had many silent conversations in my mind in which I spoke for both sides and concluded each family member considered me to be an outsider. Actually, most members of my extended family did not know about my adoption. I recall sitting and talking with my cousin whom we affectionately call "Rat." He wanted to meet my beautiful new wife, Danielle, who I was only married to for a few months at the time. As we sat and laughed about funny memories, I told him that I was adopted. He said, "Are you serious? I did not know that." Imagine the chagrin and shock on my face. I resolved everyone now knew the family's secret. Plus, I thought everyone saw the scarlet letter "A" emblazoned on my forehead. I am nearly brought to tears when I consider the countless loving celebrative occasions, times of laughter and practical jokes and just plain fun with my family members that I missed. I had charged him for an emotional crime that he did not commit and was totally unaware of. Talking about hurting people for no reason at all, this was a classic example. Not only had Almighty God embedded His unfailing and unconditional love in the hearts and character of my parents, He also put in the personalities and generosity of my extended family. Entombed within a victim's complex of abandonment and rejection as I focused upon the love that I considered lost, I failed to see the love that was right in front of me. I additionally failed to value the actual persons who were willing to share their love with me. I share this hard lesson with you because I resolved that everyone had rejected me just because of the choice of my birth parents. I allowed their decision to define my inherent worth. To heal from the rejection of family members, guard against allowing the rejection of a few persons to poison your relationships with everyone else. You risk the danger of discarding the love and genuineness of people who simply love and like you as best they can.

"When you think you are building walls to lock people out, you are really creating a prison to lock yourself in."

You may recall the biblical story of the prodigal son whose indifference to his father's unconditional love leads the son to dismiss his father and family. Demanding his total inheritance decades before it would rightly be his, the son liquidates all assets in his portfolio. He travels to a foreign land where he lives riotously and squanders his money. After his hubris results in utter humiliation, he finds himself working among pigs. In the American South, farmers call this practice in raising and feeding swine "slopping hogs." A worker takes a bucket containing bones, scraps, stale bread, apple cores, fruit skins, other discarded food items and dirty dish water to pour in a trough on top of pig feed. Precision and vigilance are necessary when "slopping hogs" as they may rise from a pool of mud, in which they have been wallowing in their urine, feces, sweat and other discharges, and shake this pungent wet dirt on the worker. Because of the potency of the smell, a thousand hot showers seem inadequate to remove it! Nonetheless, the prodigal son's refusal to accept his father's unconditional love belittled him to the point of feeding pigs as a daily occupation. His story reflects the dangerous consequence of nursing uninformed assumptions and resentments. Your ensuing isolation equates with living and working amongst pigs and livestock.

THE BLESSING OF RECONNECTING

Yet, the prodigal son's journey culminates in reconciliation with his father and family. One day, while feeding the pigs, an epiphany occurs. He finally realizes the authenticity and immensity of his father's love, which will extend forgiveness for his transgression, withdrawal and presumptions. The son returns with due humility, seeking to assume the place of a servant instead of his rightful position as a son and heir. Unimaginably, his father welcomes the son home with priceless gifts, unequivocal forgiveness and a riotous party. I doubt your story of familial abandonment and rejection will end with the words, "They lived happily ever after." Still, I exhort you to resist the fallacy of attempting to hurt others by isolating yourself. You are only damaging yourself. You will experience continuously sleepless nights, straying attention spans, physical cringes as you wonder whether anyone cares, and loss of peace of mind. In healing from abandonment and rejection within your nuclear and extended family, seeking reconciliation is the surest means of resolving your pain. You got it; this is the decision that I had to make. I had to decide to let go of the pain of an unknown past, and trade it in for the joy of a loving reality. Guess what I learned? My family loved me more than I loved myself. Wow!! Now don't look at this page and judge me. If you are rejecting people who want to love you because of fear of the unknown, then you too have allowed people to love you more than you love yourself. The only problem is, you have not accepted their love for you.

I reserved one of the most hurtful experiences of abandonment and rejection within my extended family as the last example in this chapter. I learned my paternal grandmother advised my father against adopting me because I was a sick infant. Interestingly, in an effort to demonstrate just how much he loved me; my father shared this story with me. As a consequence, I did not speak with my grandmother for nearly a decade. Her advice felt more hurtful than the initial abandonment and rejection of my birth parents. How could anyone suggest to a willingly adoptive parent that he nullify his intentions and withdraw his commitment? If I had been born physically perfect would she have given the same advice?

How could anyone be so indifferent to a helpless, defenseless and ill infant? Retroactively, her words were another betrayal. I then relegated her "love" as a deceitful act. Her consideration of me became her pity toward the human project that her son and daughter-in-law misguidedly decided to adopt against her express wishes to the contrary. It was difficult for me to believe she considered me to be a "real" grandson. My father's imprudent revelation, however well-intentioned, drove the dagger of rejection further into my heart. My anger toward my grandmother secured my entombment and isolation from the family, regardless of whether I was in their physical presence or not.

Despite my wish that my father had kept my grandmother's warning to himself, I celebrate his perseverance toward adopting me despite his mother's ironic and sincerely loving objections. I would like to believe he instantly forgave her as he experientially knew the sacred space in her heart from whence those harsh words and even crueler implications came. In time, his forgiveness of her twisted act of love enabled my forgiveness. When I first heard those words that my grandmother said as I lay in an incubator, they not only pierced my heart with abandonment and rejection, they assaulted my soul and psyche. She denied my personhood and potential because I was ill physically. She did not even consider any possibility of a miracle in healing or accomplishments in my life, and to make matters worse, she was a strong active member of the church where I now serve as Pastor. Still, God providentially sowed love for me in my father's heart. In fidelity to his love of God, my father listened to his inner voice and proceeded with adopting me. His love empowered him to surmount his mother's peculiar advice. It further encouraged him to forgive her. Consequently, my father's love eventually made my forgiveness of my grandmother possible.

A CONVERSATION THAT MADE THE DIFFERENCE

As she laid on her death bed in mid-2000 in Warrenton, North Carolina, my grandmother and I finally talked. Just for a few minutes, allow me to use your imagination. Can you see me? Here we go. Let's take a trip together so you can really see what I am saying. Walk with me into her hospital room with multiple machines, beeping noises, countless tubes, and that pervasive smell of sterility. Instead of being a place of healing and recovery, hospitals often are the final stop on life's train. As a pastor, I immediately feel the intense anxiety of congregants who have extended hospital stays. They silently and unconsciously fear that they will not leave of their own accord. When asked for a prayer request, they usually respond with discharge so that they may recuperate at home. In such a frightening setting, my grandmother and I actually reconciled. I walked in the room and when she saw me her face lit up like a Christmas tree. I did not smile one bit. She asked me, "How have you been doing? I have been trying to call you, but you never return any of my calls. I hear about all of your preaching around the country, and I have even listened to some of your sermons that your father gave me. Why have you never come to see your grandmother? What did I do to you to make you act this way towards me?" As tears flowed down her face, she appeared to be looking toward another land from which travelers never return. I said to my loving grandmother, "I heard when I was being adopted you told my father not to adopt me, so from that point on, Grandma, I decided to stay away from you since you didn't want me in the first place." Her head is now shaking from side to side as she makes a failed attempt to rise up from the bed. My mother and father quickly assist her in her effort, as I just stood there looking and waiting for her response. My anger was so bad until I remember telling my father, "I don't want to see her, just call me and let me know when she has passed away." After a brief pause, with tears in her eyes and a very trembling voice, she said to me, "Steven I love you more than you know. I only told your father that because I was scared you would not live and I did not want to see my son go through the pain of losing a child." As I was not then, and am not a parent at this writing, I could not understand fully her mother's love for my father and her sincere desire that he avoid the possibility of a parent's most fundamental loss. After all, I was a sickly infant suffering with multiple serious illnesses. My prognosis could not have been favorable initially.

> **"Quit coming to conclusions about what people think of you until you have heard it from their own mouth. If you didn't see it with your own eye, or hear it with your own ears, then don't think it with your small mind, or spread it with your big mouth."**

Chances are my grandmother was not the only person to articulate her concerns. Probably, my parents' other relatives and friends felt similarly but remained silent. As I consider these circumstances, greater gratitude and joy increase within my heart as I think of my parents completing my adoption when they, like my birth parents, could have reached for the convenient excuse of my substantive illness to withdraw their application. They had love in their hearts that surpassed my physical condition and the lack of mutual biology and genealogy. The persons with whom I shared those traits did not possess enough love to transcend the limitations with which I was born. Nevertheless, I mentally comprehended my grandmother's words within the larger setting of her limited days on Earth.

Perhaps, you may cynically characterize my grandmother's words as self-aggrandizing considering their timing and context. Within the instant of a flash of thought and emotion, I certainly did. However, death's imminence demands and coerces rigorous honesty. It extracts truth, grace and mercy from practically everyone. As my fleeting judgment evaporated into meaninglessness, my grandmother startled me, "Can you please forgive me?" As quickly as I was to dismiss her explanation, I just as quickly received divine aid to accept her request for forgiveness. I looked into her eyes as she lay on her death bed and said simply but genuinely, "Yes, Grandma." As I embraced her with a big hug, she then asked one more question, "If you forgive me, can you show me by preaching my eulogy when I pass away?" Simultaneously stunned and deeply touched by her second request, I could not deny her. In an instant, her appeal for forgiveness eliminated the chasm between us. Conceivably, had we spoken sooner, our lost decade could have witnessed ten years of an amazing relationship. I can only lament what could have been had I not entertained my victim's complex so forcefully and blamed my grandmother for her seminal contribution in rejecting me. What a ferocious and furious volcano the ego within a wounded person can be? How the lava of righteous indignation spews forth fluidly condemning anyone suspected of compounding your pain and consuming every relationship as tainted with betrayal and deceit! Be that as it may, with great pride and authenticity, I preached the eulogy at my grandmother's funeral with tremendous joy. I am truly thankful we spoke and reconciled before her transition to eternal life.

In the 1992 movie, *A River Runs Through It*, directed by Robert Redford and starring Brad Pitt and Tom Skerritt, a Presbyterian minister struggles with the death of his younger son, whom the minister resolves he never really understood, and thus was unable to help in overcoming the prodigality that resulted in the son's untimely death. Ruminating within the deep recesses of the minister's mind and heart, the minister agonizes over an explanation of his son's death and his inability to assist his son. In a sermon he delivers shortly before his own death, the Presbyterian minister profoundly posits, after acknowledging the hard and inexplicable reality of our powerlessness to help those persons who are closest to us emotionally and relationally, "We can love completely without complete understanding." This quote summarizes my heartfelt feelings and resolution relating to my grandmother. Perhaps, neither she nor I really understood each other, but we had a chance to love each other. Love does not require complete comprehension of another human being. Really, who amongst any of us understands himself? Life is a perpetual and progressive process of self-discovery and understanding. As we require and expect patience and forbearance of loved ones and friends, we extend the same consideration and tolerance to them. Otherwise, we commit the unpardonable sin of condemning in other people the sins that we so easily forgive within ourselves. Summarily, I encourage you to embrace genuine forgiveness as your best method of overcoming abandonment and rejection from family.

In an incredible book on forgiveness, *To Forgive is Human: How to Put Your Past in the Past*,[2] Everett L. Worthington suggests stories that contain intrinsic healing power. My previous summary of the story of the prodigal son attests to Worthington's point. Practically, everyone identifies with the prodigality of the young son and also sees a reflection of his own profligacy in that biblical character. I hope my story of frankness, anger, distance and reconciliation with my grandmother offers hope to you as you heal from any rejection you experienced within your immediate and extended family. My grandmother's plea that I forgive her healed the hurt I felt for a decade. Her sincere request yielded my equally genuine forgiveness of her. Forgiveness, the redemptive and transformative act of repudiating your right to retribution and punishment, is the main source of healing within ruptured human relationships. I hasten to add that honesty, dignity and respect are necessary to exchange forgiveness. Victims and victimizers must honor each other with truth thereby respecting each other's inherent human dignity and worth. Furthermore, forgiveness is a selfish act. In extending forgiveness to a victimizer, victims liberate themselves from imprisonment to anger, fear, resentment, bitterness, strife and other toxic emotions. Refusal to forgive entombs the victim to an existential death whereby he physically and externally relates to people but inwardly and emotionally he extinguishes all relationships because of his inherent distrust of everyone. Within his mind and heart, he kills any possibility of a meaningful and rewarding relationship as he fears additional betrayal and pain. Forgiveness recalls the victim to life and resurrects him to a new way of relating to people.

HOW DO YOU FORGIVE?

Honesty, open-mindedness and willingness are three practical components of forgiveness. As the people who hurt you admit their actions without equivocation, they create willingness for forgiveness. Willingness in turn opens your heart and mind to new mysteries, joy and experiences in relationships. As you increasingly learn to forgive, specifically family members who rejected you, let them love you as they are capable. Though you cannot choose your family, you can give and receive genuine love with them. My experience in my grandmother's hospital room reminds me of the necessity of loving people each day. Forsake righteous indignation and ingratiating your ego, it is better to live in right relationship with people than to be right. Broken relationships heal organically when people invest in rebuilding them. Just because people do not express their love for you in your preferred love language does not mean they do not love you. Human beings cannot perfectly express their love as they are not perfect. Consistent, respectful and clear communication yield love, forgiveness and reconciliation.

"When you ask God to forgive you of your errors, then it only follows that you are expected to forgive people who have committed errors towards you. Don't look for forgiveness if you yourself are unwilling to be forgiving toward others."

UNCONDITIONAL LOVE

I married my wife and was quickly introduced to a family who shares love in a wonderful way. Let me be clear, my family does the same, but I shut myself out so early until I was unable to appreciate the love that was extended. Have you ever wondered how other families love so easily but it seems so hard in your family? The answer is simple…you are probably more open and vulnerable to others because you have not been hurt by them. This is what happened to me. I found myself enjoying spending more time with her family than my own. It took a while for me to see that the love that is observed in the Frank family is the same love that is available in the Carter family. Nothing is worse than not accepting the love that you are being extended.

However, God is so gracious until he has allowed me to see the love in her family and accept the love from my own. Since being married to my wife, I have opened up more to my family. I have done things such as *call more often, take time to visit people, treat family members to dinners, listen to family stories that I never heard, ask questions that I have been scared of, etc.* As a result, I learned that it was not my family who was rejecting me…it was me who was rejecting my family. If you are in this space in your journey, quit asking questions that keep you disconnected from your family, and start asking questions and doing things that will pull you closer to you family. Remember, when family is gone, you will not be able to make-up for lost time. Make it your business to get connected to your family, even if it is not everyone, get connected to the people who you know care deeply for and about you. I did it, and you can do it too!

"Family means no one gets left behind or forgotten." –David Ogden Stiers[3]

7 WAYS TO LOVE YOUR FAMILY

1. Learn to give thanks for your family and love them accordingly.

2. Learn to forgive in a timely manner and seek reconciliation with family members.

3. Learn to humble yourself and receive your family member's love as they give genuinely and generously.

4. Learn to be open to your family, love them, as they change and grow with you.

5. Be open-minded about love, particularly from people who previously hurt you.

6. Let people love you as they are able.

7. Communicate, verbally and non-verbally, your love for your family

REVIEW QUESTIONS

What is your definition of family?

_____

_____

Have you ever been treated in a way that made you feel as if you were not important to your family?

☐ All the time

☐ A few times

☐ Never

☐ Can't remember

List three of your family members other than your parents and siblings who you are extremely close to? After you list them, if they do not know that you appreciate their closeness, make sure you reach out and connect with them.

_____

_____

_____

Have you ever been told something about yourself from a family member that was negative and you have not been able to get it out of your head? If yes, please write it out.

☐ Yes: _____

_____

☐ No

If you have ever withdrawn from your family because of feelings of rejection, in which ways did you withdraw?

☐ Stayed away from family events

☐ Do not call as often as I used to

☐ Stop talking to my family completely

☐ Other: _____

_____

_____

Are there some people who you would like to reconnect with in your family? If so, please write their names down and set a date by which you will contact them. If by chance you are worried about their response, just reconnect and if they do not receive you, do not take it personally.

Their name is: _____

_____

_____

As with my grandmother, is there someone you need to forgive and talk to before time runs out? If yes, write their name(s).

☐ Yes: _____

_____

☐ No

ENDNOTES

1   Tutu, Desmond. As quoted in *Families Torn Apart: Human Rights and US Restrictions on Cuban-Americans Travel* – Hearings Before the Subcommittee on International Organizations, Human Rights and Oversight of the Committee on Foreign Affairs, United States House of Representatives, One Hundred Tenth Congress, Second Session, September 18, 2008, Volume 4, pp.8-9.

2   Worthington, Everett L. *To Forgive Is Human: How to Put Your Past in The Past* (Downers Grove, Illinois: Inter-Varsity Press, 1997).

3   Stiers, David Ogden as quoted in Reco McDaniel. *The Fatherless Father: The Life Story of Reco McDaniel* (published ebook format – http://www.eBookIt.com Conyers, GA, 2012, Chapter 13).

HEALING 3
YOU ARE LIKEABLE: HEALING FROM REJECTION BY FRIENDS

"A friend is someone who knows you and loves you just the same." —Elbert Hubbard[1]

THE DANGER OF CHOOSING BAD FRIENDS

Have you ever selected some bad friends to hang out with? I sure did. In 1990, while a student at Washington Irving High School in Manhattan, I joined a local train gang. I remember it clearly! We used to ride the #4 train from Manhattan to Brooklyn every day. As a consequence of feeling rejected, I entered wrong and unproductive relationships. Eventually, my gang membership led to my expulsion. I then attended one of the most dangerous schools in Brooklyn, Thomas Jefferson High School. If you live in Brooklyn, then you already know about TJHS. In 1992, two students were murdered during the school day. After being shot to death, probably by another young man who did not know how to receive or give love, their bodies literally laid on the second floor. As the school's reputation was so notorious, the police and administration simply sealed off the second floor and continued school as a usual day. Death was so common until dismissal was not an option, just closure to the second floor. The sad truth is the community of East New York had become so numb to death and evil that the murders of those adolescents were not a sufficient reason to close the school.

I realize patterns of behavioral dysfunction had formed within my character by the time I joined that gang in my previous school. Beyond the usual peer pressure with which high school students contend, the affects and effects of parental and familial rejection led to my entrance into a gang. I needed somewhere to belong. I wanted a group of people to welcome me in their midst simply because I am Steven. I desperately desired to belong relationally without the trappings of whether I was a "real" son versus an adopted one. I sought to evade the conditions that I felt had been placed upon my worth. If gang members saw me as an equal, then they would not care whether I was adopted. They would treat me as they would anyone else who belonged to the group. Simply, my self-esteem was so low that I was willing to belong to any group of persons who led me to believe that they accepted me without conditions. The anger and disillusionment resulting from learning of my adoption made gang membership an appealing option.

"Before you look to be accepted by others, be thankful that you are accepted by God, then learn how to be accepting of yourself."

The beliefs and activities of a gang contradicted my core moral values and personal principles. I found no pleasure in intimidating people. I was not a sadist who drooled as fear consumed another person who fears he risks bodily injury or greater danger. I recall the glee on the faces of fellow gang members as they watched fear form on the faces of soon-to-be victims. I remember how empowered they felt as we walked away with the loot of muggings, robberies and other petty offenses. In retrospect, I know I deeply desired friendship as I always valued the possibility of being in relationship with persons who simply like you without cause or conditions. Friends do not judge each other. They do not make each other submit to pedigree and other litmus tests. Loyalty and perseverance are foundational to good friendships. Gangs create and maintain a veneer of genuine friendship. Behind the veil, manipulation, exploitation, confusion and identity crises perpetuate gang membership. When someone wants desperately to belong, he may join any organization. Cults, supremacist groups and other terrorist organizations recruit vulnerable persons who seek assurance and confidence. Young, impressionable and desiring acceptance, I compromised my beliefs and joined that gang. Yet, genuine friendship was my sole objective.

PUTTING ON A FAKE FRONT

I was the type of person who always kept my friends feeling comfortable with opening themselves to me, though I hardly ever really disclosed my inner self to them. I suffered with intimacy anxiety as I did not think I could trust anyone after my parents held such a significant secret from me for thirteen years. My insecurity made me approach people only if I thought I could benefit from an exchange with them. I would not allow anyone else to burn me again. I already had enough people in my life who had caused me considerable pain. Fiercely, I guarded against any possibility of additional instances of abandonment. My biological parents saw me and probably instantly loved me until they realized how sick I was. Then, they forthrightly, and seemingly unrepentantly, abandoned me. As an adolescent, I resolved that no other human being would possess that type of power over me. I would not allow anyone to know me as I feared being abandoned again. My image of myself as a broken, irreparable person who could not earn the love and loyalty of his parents made me suspect that everyone else viewed me in a similar way. Accordingly, I overcompensated by appearing as if I was always in total control of every situation. An egomaniac with an inferiority complex and a deep-seated identity crisis, I was not teachable. I knew everything. I would not admit to any limitations or ignorance, despite the reality of their existence. I walked through daily life with a humongous chip on my shoulder. Now, I realize myriad ways in which my perfectionism alienated and repelled people. Moreover, my insecurities prevented any possibility of authentic friendships with anyone. Average people do not have the time or inclination to boulder through my petrified defense mechanisms. One of the many things that Dr. Joe Samuel Ratliff shared with me when I joined his staff that remains in my mind was, "Be who you are and quit trying to look and act like people think you should act." Those words really helped me because I was always conditioned to act and look a certain way, especially as someone who was called into my profession. I encourage you to do the same, be who you are and your life will flow a lot easier.

Ok, let me continue with what I was saying. *In its simplest form, friendship exists between two or more people who share common interests, values, humor, experiences, and outlooks upon life.* Similarly situated as it relates to social, economic, and political characteristics, friends usually do not have expectations of each other. To put another way, real friends are willing to accept people for where they are and grow together as one benefits from the other without the other feeling like they are only being drained of their energy, time and/or finances. Friends are able to relate to each other freely as they seek to gain from the relationship in a mutual way. As equals, they can exchange ideas, information and confidentiality as they do not risk manipulation or extortion. A presumption of progressive self-acceptance and mutual respect enable longstanding friendships. Friends willingly expect support and encouragement from each other as they seek to give the same in return.

Therefore, it stands to reason that friends must have genuine self-acceptance. Jealousy, greed and hidden motives prevent friendship. Mutual respect eliminates "people pleasing" demands. Friends do not perform for each other or maintain appearances. Morality and ethics of friendship prevent social, economic and collective manipulation. Generally, friendship is not a means of upward social and economic mobility. Friendship is an existential space where a person shares openly, gives freely and securely enjoys companionship without fear of reprisal, resentment or ulterior motives. This ideal is attainable between persons who equally and progressively enjoy self-acceptance.

> *"Connect with people who are going places and stay away from people whose lives seem to always be stuck in complaints and bitterness."*

Naively, I considered my gang membership as a collective friendship. No one in the group possessed self-acceptance. We were very broken and frightened individuals hoping to combine the pieces of our personalities into a whole one. Rather than empowering each other, our allegiance served to impede our individual growth and emotional maturity. Frankly, we were using each other to make ourselves feel better. Our adolescent rituals and concerns seemed significant as the gang gave a voice and place to belong. Whereas we felt like misfits in all other areas of life, belonging to our gang supplied a refuge from insecurity, intimidation, and indirection.

DESPERATE APPROVAL LEADS TO DESPERATE CHOICES

Broken and hurt people who are feeling unloved has also caused people to jump into marriages very soon, thinking that the marriage will heal the wound. I suspect failed marriages between persons in their late teens and early twenties understandably occur as these persons do not know enough about themselves as individuals to decide and commit to a challenging and lifelong covenant. Possibly, a chance conversation in which two broken and hurt persons empathize with each other's pain and heartache leads them to believe they can heal each other within a committed relationship. They extend a potentially good friendship into a relationship by acting on their favorable emotions through having sex which then coerces them to commit exclusively to each other. In time, they formalize their serial monogamy in marriage with religious ritual and a legally binding contract. However, the church ceremony, religious covenant and state contract do not alter the complex and difficult emotions of two very immature persons who are still growing up and learning about life. Eventually, they face the harsh realities that they actually share very little in common other than a sincere desire to heal from the pain and brokenness of childhood. As they progress to their middle to late twenties, they feel as if they have courage and strength to face the world alone and discover what it has to offer to them as individuals. They embrace and thank each other for their kindness and help over the course of the few years that comprised their marriage. Naturally, they separate and divorce as their shared emotional and familial brokenness was not enough to sustain a marriage or build a genuine friendship. This is not to say that young marriages cannot last. My parents married young, and 49 years later, they are still together. What I am saying is that sometimes when people are broken, they look for love at a young age to make an attempt to connect with someone who loves them, or who they think can make up for the love that they have been lacking and searching to find for many years.

Lest I glamorize friendships, I hasten to admit it is often the source of remarkable, inexplicable and pervasive betrayal and deceit. The most common instance of betrayal in Western culture is Judas Iscariot's disloyalty to Jesus Christ in exchange for thirty pieces of silver. As a member of the inner circle of the Jesus movement and treasurer of the twelve disciples, Judas is close enough to Christ to betray Him. Enemies cannot deceive us as we rarely allow them close proximity. Most definitely, we do not allow them access to the inner chambers of our thoughts, consciousness and character. Because we trust them, friends are able to deceive and hurt us. Their betrayal equates with rejection. If they continually value us and our friendship, they would not injure us. Betrayal from friends particularly hurts as oftentimes we are closer to friends than we are to relatives. In keeping with the theme of this book, I ask the question, "How do we heal from rejection by friends?"

Though you may not view people with my previous suspicion and ulterior motives, chances are you have had your experiences with betrayal by persons whom you thought were your friends. Interestingly, as I grew up and joined the gang, I learned separately about the components of true friendship from my father. He always admonished me, "Boy, be very careful about your choice of friends." My parents wanted to know everything about anyone I called a friend. Who are their parents? What church do they attend? Constantly, they asked these and other questions. In retrospect, I appreciate their inquiries and intrusiveness as they kept me from many unknown troubles. My parents taught me with their example the truth of the enduring adage: If you have one true friend, you are lucky; and if you have more than one, you have received a miracle. In my life I have been blessed with many friends, but one in particular who has been, and continues to be, like a brother to me is my good friend and brother, Jawanza Colvin. He and I share in the same vocation as Pastor. We established an unbreakable bond during our years at Morehouse College. Needless to say, our friendship has grown to the point where we have celebrated wonderful lifelong memories together. I was privileged to be the Best Man in his wedding, and I was honored to have him as the Best Man in mine. I thank God for his friendship. It's a blessing that not many can claim.

Another great example of friendship that helped me learn more about family love was formed during my time in seminary. I was in Durham, North Carolina away from family, but was able to connect with a fellow Morehouse Graduate, Michael Walrond. Interesting enough, he and I are both serving as Pastors in New York City. During my seminary days I was able to work with him at the church where he formerly served as Pastor, but I was also allowed into the comfort of his family. There were many great family experiences that he allowed me to share with his wife Lakeesha, children (Tre & Jazmine), his mother, and other extended family members. I remember coming home one vacation and being invited to have dinner with his family in Long Island, New York. Keep in mind, I had my own family in New York, but because I did not feel as connected, I quickly took this opportunity. It was a time when I could get away and be around people who did not pre-label me as the non-family member. Not only did I develop a bond with his side of the family, but I was also introduced to Lakeesha's mother, who accepted me as family and always came to support me whenever I was preaching in her city, Houston, Texas. Please know that to many people, these may not seem like major moments, but to me, it meant the world and more because it told me this one thing: There are people who genuinely love and support you and will not reject you. To this day Mike & Keesha continue to remain like family to me, and it's a bond that will continue without termination.

> *"If you value true friendships based on how often you speak with someone, then your friendships will always be seasonal and never life-time."*

It is always necessary and important that a victim of pain, deceit and injury examine any role he may have played in causing his misfortune. It seems cruel to ask victims of violent crimes and extreme financial scams to assess what they may have done to contribute to their situation. However, they can learn from the experience and utilize their lessons as empowerment and encouragement as they heal and find "a new normal." Being more vigilant about their safety or taking self-defense classes will liberate a victim from being a perpetual victim. A victim of greed, like that of Madoff's Ponzi scheme, inevitably wrestles with his own greed that laid dormant within his character as he accepts that he believed the unrealistic and impractical earnings potential because he wanted to get rich quick. Self-examination is an important aspect in developing daily spiritual discipline leading toward holistic self-acceptance. As you internalize the divine wisdom and biblical teachings of Psalm 139, specifically verses thirteen through sixteen, you begin to see yourself as God sees you. There is nothing intrinsically wrong with you. You are fearfully and wonderfully made. God created you in His image to reflect His divinity, majesty and love. God gave you a unique personality that attracts as many persons as it repels. The people who are drawn to you are interested potentially in becoming your friend or desire to have association with you for other reasons. For whatever arbitrary and unknown reasons, the people who dislike you will not be able to reverse their opinion of you. There is very little that you can do to alter their assessment of you. Nevertheless, as you more forthrightly accept, approve, love and esteem yourself, you attract genuine friends who appreciate and celebrate you because you freely accept and express your unique character and personality. Essentially, you heal from rejection and betrayal by friends as you invest in self-acceptance, enabling you to choose better friends.

Centered upon historic tourist attractions in Washington, DC, the nation's capital, Margaret Truman's murder mysteries often embed the strongest and most revealing clues within a conversation. To figure out who committed the murder, readers must play close attention to any dialogue between central characters. Interestingly, most good, genuine and growing friendships usually begin with a chance conversation in which one person risks and shares significant personal challenges. Any mature recipient of another person's confidence and raw feelings responds with respectful gratitude and keeps the confidence. In time, he opens his mind and heart to share equally important personal experiences. Lifelong friendships are the result. As friendships grow, people challenge and encourage each other to become the best children of God of which they are capable. A friend of mine immensely helped me to grow and heal. He would not allow me to wallow endlessly in my victim's complex of abandonment and rejection resulting from my adoption. He sharply exhorted me, "Go on with your life."

I will never forget the day of my greatest excitement and disappointment. I was supposed to meet my biological parents for the first time. Time and location was scheduled, and I was preparing everything that I would say to them. I wanted to ask questions, see how they look, check out some medical facts, and so much more. However, the day that started off sunny, quickly became cloudy for me. Yes, you already guessed it. My parents did not show up to meet the son who they abandoned at birth. Once again, I gave them a chance and they left me hanging. I was mad at them and myself. Mad at them for not showing up, and mad at myself for giving them the chance to not show up. I should have simply stayed where I was and just left everything a mystery. Later that evening, I tried to ease my pains by going to hear a renowned preacher who is also like a big brother to me. After hearing him give a great sermon, as always, we hung out so I could pick his brains about ministry and life. This time was a little different, I just wanted to vent, and he was the lucky candidate. Our talk in the car after service occurred during an emotional binge of revenge in which I longed for my biological parents to feel the same pain and hurt I remember. I started telling him about my day and how I wanted my biological parents to experience the exact trials and tribulations that I had. I wanted to be sure they were sorry for what they had done. Were they aware of the misery I suffered because of their selfishness? I felt as if they were fugitives who successfully escaped justice. I was going off and complaining about my day and letting him know that I wanted to hurt my parents tremendously. I said to him, "I really want to see them so I can hurt their feelings and let them see what a great son they missed out on." As my "Big Bro" listened to my ranting and raving, the words that would come out of his mouth were words that I was not prepared to hear. Guess what he said to me as I sat with great frustration? ARE YOU READY? I don't think you are. He told me, "You can't hurt their feelings; they are the ones who gave you up at birth." I was ready to hit him in the back of his head, but I was not crazy! I realized at that moment that I am powerless to make another person feel any type of emotion, let alone guilt, shame, regret or humiliation. After relinquishing the feeling of wanting to respond with a barrage of profanity, I realized my Big Bro words created a moment of truth. I had to let go of the useless emotions of desiring revenge upon my biological parents. I could not make them feel remorse for their decision. My success since their abandonment could not compel them to rethink their decision. My whole life lay before me. I had to choose to live up to my fullest potential.

> ## "Truth hurts, but usually the truth that hurts the most is often the truth that will bring the most healing."

In addition, my Big Bro helped me to realize that my quest for punishment and perpetual resentment was harming me. I was giving power to my biological parents to define me as irreversibly broken and constitutionally incapable of growth and change. My resentments confirmed my worst fears and their decision to abandon me. As I nursed my revenge, I reaffirmed my worthlessness in their eyes and even mine. At that moment, I resolved that I would no longer analyze their decision. Regardless of whatever explanation anyone offers, I am unable to agree with it. Accordingly, I chose on that night, and continue to this day, to accept and celebrate the parents whom God gave me through the mystical, mysterious and providential orchestration of adoption. I would maximize each opportunity life presents daily. Mostly, I would love my parents, extended family and friends. I would no longer waste energy seeking vengeance upon persons who rejected, abandoned and isolated me. Instead, I would appreciate the people who enrich my life and accept me as I am. My big bro's bold words of tough love opened a door to a new and rewarding life for me. Our conversation demonstrates the endless possibilities of genuine and caring friendships to be instruments of grace and healing after experiencing betrayal and broken relationships.

TEMPORARY FORGIVENESS

Guess what? My forgiveness did not last long. I fell back into the state of not forgiving my parents. My empowering breakthrough came when I had another conversation that I will cherish always. This conversation occurred at a cigar bar in Manhattan when I visited with Pastor Ralph Douglas West. He had just finished preaching at the church where I serve as Pastor. We were excited simply to share time together as mentor and mentee. In the course of the conversation, I shared how upset I was because my biological parents did not show up to see me for the first time. It felt as if they were rejecting me again. After all, I had given them another chance to make things right. They had an opportunity to tell me that they had made a mistake. My overwhelming emotions felt like I was starring in a recurring nightmare. Really, deep within me, I harbored the thirst to see them in order to hurt them and make them feel the pain I felt. I wanted them to see the healthy, successful, educated and increasingly prosperous son whom they relegated to the trash pile of humankind. After finishing my tirade, I paused for Pastor West's reactions and thoughts. He began by recommending that I read a book, *Forgive and Forget*, by Smedes[2]. "It will really help you live through your pain." Still, Pastor West continued to listen and slowly nod his head, as is his manner. You never really know whether he agrees with you or whether he says silently to himself, "This dude is really losing his mind." Considerately, Pastor West did not rebuke me, laugh at my pain or otherwise fail to appreciate my struggle in forgiving my biological parents. He lovingly and wisely encouraged me to forgive my biological parents and move on with my life. Admittedly, it remains a simplistic but a significant suggestion. Furthermore, Pastor West offered a transformative perspective on parenthood from an adopted son's view. He reiterated my need to forgive the parents who gave birth to me and then left for reasons only known to them. Pastor West then recommended, "Steven, your biological parents are Mr. Eugene and Mrs. Mary Carter. From this day forward, stop referring to them as your adopted parents. How would you feel if they always referred to you as their adopted son?" His distinction felt as if a ton of bricks had fallen on me. Throughout my life, I characterized my parents in a way that created distance between us. As I labeled them my "adoptive parents," I unconsciously accepted the idea that they were not my "real" parents. In ways, I was agreeing with the wrongful notion that they were doing me a favor. I was a personified charitable project and not a son. They were nice, giving people but not my parents who loved me unconditionally.

As I write, I relive this pivotal moment which parallels the removal of the tombstone at Lazarus' grave. Pastor West's suggestion equates with Jesus calling Lazarus forth from the grave. My mentor's words encouraged and empowered me to discard the image of myself as a victim who happened to receive the liberal largesse of Christian parents. Transcending biology, legacy, genealogy and history, I am a son with loving parents! Although I was not dead physically, for so many years, I was dead emotionally. At that precise moment, I heard the Lord say to me, "Steven, get out of your grave of rejection and come forth and live the life I gave you."

YOU CAN LIVE AGAIN

Perhaps, you have an area in your life where you are emotionally dead. God is calling you to come forth and live. Perhaps you have been in that space for such a lengthy period that you cannot hear His voice or imagine a different way of living. It is time to experience resurrection from your grave of rejection, betrayal and abandonment. As you heal from rejection by friends, you will receive God's favor in the person of someone who like Pastor West will cross your path to offer words of inspiration, hope and encouragement. If you cannot think of anyone, I ask you to consider me as that person. I believe you are not reading this book as a coincidence. It is an answer to your quest for inner healing and wholeness. As God is not a respecter of persons and will do for you what He did for me, and even more, the fact that you are reading this book means you will, in fact, experience resurrection from rejection.

The two foregoing conversations reflect the potential of good and growing friendships to provide healing and recovery from past pain. I hope you will receive grace to encounter someone with a similar background. You will have someone who can relate to your feelings and thus will not judge you or attempt to dismiss your pain. As you share with this person, listen without judging him. As you empathize with each other, you will find spiritual power to heal. Someone who traveled through the valley of the shadow of death can lead another fearful traveler through its tough terrain. The recovery community advocates sponsorship as a reliable means of achieving and maintaining sobriety. A fellow alcoholic and friend has experiential knowledge about the steps of sobriety. His suggestions trump book knowledge on any day. I assume such a role for you as I share my story with you. On the authority of my experience of resurrection from rejection, I unequivocally assure you that healing and a new life await you. Consider me your friend. I am more than another author who aspired to write a book. I am a man who seeks to share God's love. As we travel together know that there is no hurt that God cannot heal.

In a sense, we walk along the road to Emmaus on the first Easter Sunday. Luke records the story of Cleopas and a fellow disciple as they leave Jerusalem in bitter grief, immeasurable disillusionment and inconceivable hopelessness. They invested in the Jesus movement. They thought that Jesus of Nazareth was the One who would restore Israel to her former glory. They were certain that He was the Messiah for whose coming their people had prayed for centuries. Three days following Jesus's crucifixion, Cleopas and the nameless disciple decide to return to their former life in Emmaus. Prior to leaving Jerusalem, they ironically hear an account of the resurrection. Still, they continue their journey back to Emmaus. As they walk along the road, a stranger inexplicably joins them. He listens to their feelings and disappointment. As the fog of their grief pervades their minds and hearts, they are unable to recognize the Risen Lord Jesus Christ. He walks beside them and discloses divine mysteries to them beginning with the Old Testament Law and Prophets. Their hearts burn as they listen to Him. Bear in mind that they are walking toward the sunset of a closing day and toward nightfall in a familiar place. As dusk approaches, the three of them stop for a meal. As they begin to eat, the scales fall from their eyes and they recognize the Lord. Their companionship enables them to support each other as they encounter and experience God's healing presence and power. Genuine friendship is one of God's most effective means of restoration. I hope and pray this book is a beginning for you.

In summary, God walked beside Cleopas and his unnamed companion as they journeyed toward the sunset of disappointment and disillusionment and redirected them toward the sunrise of a new life at the dusk of the first Easter. He turned their course around. Rather than settling for sunset and night's darkness, they reversed course and headed back toward the dawn of resurrection. In genuine friendships, God provides words and wisdom of new life.

"Lots of people want to ride with you in the limo, but what you want is someone who will take the bus with you when the limo breaks down." —Oprah Winfrey[3]

I OFFER FIVE HELPFUL HINTS FOR CHOOSING GENUINE FRIENDS.

1. Choose people who accept you as you are.

2. Choose people who genuinely celebrate you, your gifts and your blessings.

3. Choose people who commit to you and invest in your friendship.

4. Choose people who are positive and affirm other people.

5. Choose people who accept themselves, believe in themselves and continually challenge themselves to develop personally and grow spiritually.

IN ADDITION, I SUGGEST YOU AVOID THESE FIVE TYPES OF PEOPLE.

1. Avoid people who are negative, cynical and complain.

2. Avoid people who are incapable of telling the truth and standing for a just outcome.

3. Avoid people who lack morality, ethics and integrity.

4. Avoid people who are incapable of standing with you in difficult times.

5. Avoid people with questionable characters.

REVIEW QUESTIONS

Who are your top 5 closest friends?

_____

_____

_____

Are there some friends or associates in your circle who you know you need to eliminate from your life? Make sure that you do not allow your FEELINGS to interrupt your FUTURE. If there are some people you need to eliminate or be around less, write their names here.

I need to pull away from:

_____

_____

Are you able to be yourself around your friends?

☐ Yes

☐ Sometimes

☐ No

☐ Depends on the day

In what ways have you looked for approval or validation in your life?

☐ From parents & siblings

☐ From peers

☐ From co-workers

☐ Other: _____

_____

Have you ever told someone you FORGAVE them but you really did not mean it? If so, write their name down and make it your business to forgive them in your heart, God is able to help you be victorious.

_____

_____

_____

Regardless of your past, do you really believe that your future can be better?

☐ Yes

☐ I have doubts

☐ Not at all

☐ I don't know

☐ I will make it better

ENDNOTES

1   Hubbard, Elbert.   http://www.brainyquote.com/quotes/authors/e/elbert_hubbard.html

2   Smedes, Lewis B. *Forgive and Forget: Healing the Hurts We Don't Deserve* (New York: Harper One, 1996).

3   Winfrey, Oprah.   http://www.brainyquote.com/quotes/quotes/o/oprahwinfr105255.html

HEALING 4
YOU ARE LOVABLE: HEALING FROM FAILED RELATIONSHIPS

"To love oneself is the beginning of a lifelong romance." –Oscar Wilde[1]

REJECTED PEOPLE RUN AWAY FROM BEING LOVED

As a result of feeling rejected, I never allowed myself to fall in love or experience authentic, intimate relationships. Actually, I did not fall in love until I met my wonderful wife Danielle. I found her to be so amazing that I told myself, "I am not going to allow my fears to keep me from the love that I know I can receive and offer." My wife's loving, caring, gentle and generous personality overwhelmed the walls of my defense mechanisms. Love truly conquers pain, suffering, injustice and betrayal. Ultimately, love heals rejection, brokenness, failure and abandonment. God's unfailing love for humankind resurrected Jesus from the dead, thereby offering eternal life to anyone who believes. For you, personally, His steadfast love can transform your past hurt and heartache into a unique ability to forgive, accept yourself and love selflessly.

However, life teaches us that we can love the wrong person. The neo-orthodox theologian, Paul Tillich, one of the foremost religious thinkers of the twentieth century, interprets the story of Mary anointing Jesus with an expensive jar of perfume and wiping His feet with her hair as an example of God's lavish waste of His love in Christ upon humankind. From the infidelity of Adam and Eve in the Garden of Eden, to the building of a golden calf by the wilderness generation, to the murder of the prophets, to the crucifixion of Jesus, humankind steadfastly squanders God's love. Though He creates us in His image to reflect His love and character (Psalm 8), God receives humankind's unrequited love. Mary's incredible and incalculable act of gratitude demonstrates how costly genuine love is. It further shows how hurtful and demoralizing it is when you love someone who fails to respect you and tramples upon your emotions, kindnesses and commitment. Rejection from unreciprocated love and failed relationships hurts worse than any other type of pain. Perhaps, you have loved the wrong person. Healing from divorce, broken engagements or abusive, verbal and physical relationships resembles the pain of rejection and abandonment. Still, you can experience resurrection from those difficult and hard experiences.

"If you are scared to risk being hurt by someone, then you will never get the chance to be loved by someone."

FROM ONE RELATIONSHIP TO THE NEXT

Constantly shifting relationships is one way of avoiding self-pity, doubt, insecurity, anger, resentment, fear and unrequited love that follows when someone takes advantage of you and your heart. One of the reasons that I never allowed myself to fall in love was my fear of emotional rejection. It seemed safer to sidestep this risk. It was much easier and safer to just get to know someone, date them, then end it before my heart was positioned to be broken or rejected. I did not wish to add to the mountain of rejection that I was already climbing. I made fear larger than life. I would not risk love to avoid being hurt repeatedly. I could not stomach another rejection, particularly from a young woman whom I sought to impress. True for many people, I ran away from love because I was scared to love. Tennyson's adage, "Tis' better to have loved and lost than never to have loved at all,"[2] held no promise for me. My cumulative experience of abandonment and rejection negated his wisdom. As a consequence of my unresolved feelings of identity, acceptance and esteem, I compensated with multiple temporary relationships.

I knew the sayings and strategies to attract most women. One woman actually told me during my dating days, "I was really not into you, but the way you held good conversation just made me want to talk to you a little more, and before I knew it, I was liking you." Needless to say, I knew what I was doing the entire time. The goal was to always get into someone's head, because this did not involve my heart with emotions. It only pulled on my ability to use intellect without any major emotional risk. However, I also knew how to control my emotions and prevent myself from falling in love with anyone. Regrettably, I benefited at the expense of several women's emotions and dignity. I used them, not in an evil way, but to offer me a relationship that I knew would not lead to love as I prevailed through my pain. Regardless of my neglect of my own emotions, I was always respectful towards who I was dating. I guess that was what really made it strange. I treated the person as if I were "here to stay," but I knew in my heart that this was only a temporary relationship. I took their consideration, compassion, comfort, and hope for granted; satisfying my ego and physical instincts. My childhood trauma justified the pain and heartache I caused other people in my life. Inevitably, as the victim of unrequited love, you relish the opportunity to make someone feel the same pain you felt. Being rejected, I acted in ways that I did not realize would result in the rejection of others. I began to treat others in the same manner that I felt I was treated. Unknowingly, I utilized my horrific experience as a license to use and mistreat other people. I lived in a bubble in which I convinced myself, "Hurt or be hurt." Accepting such limiting beliefs as, "No one will really love you because your own parents failed to love you," I did not allow myself to feel love or any other pure emotion.

LEARN TO LOVE YOURSELF FIRST

I did not fall in love until I began to resolve my issues of abandonment and rejection. I had to learn how to love me. I had to let go of the image of myself as an irreparably sick, broken and worthless child whose parents looked away from and abandoned. I could not want love to complete me. I could not expect someone to rescue me. I could not hold another person responsible for my healing and self-worth. I had to face my fears. I had to find courage and willingness to be vulnerable. I was so deep in my pain from the past fear of rejection until I did not give second chances. A person would cross, disappoint or betray me once. I did not tolerate disloyalty. These primal feelings stem from my experience with abandonment and rejection. Disappointment from family members and friends is particularly hard. Yet, denial from someone who interests you romantically is even harder. If I sensed any possibility that a woman was leading me on, I immediately withdrew from her and any chance of a relationship. If I thought she was planning on breaking up with me or altering what I assumed we had, I hastened the termination of our relationship, or whatever it was. I did not want to be abandoned and rejected again. My underlying feelings of self-doubt and self-pity would not allow me to experience the trauma of being left, yet again, by someone whom I expected to love me. I realize my deep-rooted insecurity created patterns of thoughts in my consciousness, decision-making in my choices, and behavior in my character. I unconsciously accepted the limiting beliefs of being unlovable and worthless so much so that I tried to eliminate the idea of love altogether. I worked hard to perfect an outward persona that demanded respect and consideration from other people. Specifically, I assumed women would find my humor appealing. I seriously expected them to be attracted to the brother who could make them laugh without ever revealing my own insecurities. Some of them were emotionally healthy enough to detect my ingrained patterns of fear and low self-esteem. They wanted to be in relationship with another person, not a project to repair. I remember one person I dated said these words to me, "I really thank God for you, but He surely gave me a project that seems impossible." Needless to say, I cut her off because I sensed that my days were numbered in her mind. Therefore, being absolutely tired of the Herculean burden of feeling rejected, I attempted to prevent any further possible rejection through unrequited love by ending a relationship before she would.

"If you cannot change the people around you, then maybe you need to change the people around you."

Unrequited love – the phenomenon of loving someone who cannot and does not reciprocate your feelings – considerably parallels abandonment and rejection. It is very difficult to resist personalizing unrequited love, even in instances when someone respects you and honors your dignity by sharing in a timely way and in honesty that he or she does not share your thoughts and emotions. Unrequited love affects self-esteem and identity. Questions immediately form in your mind. What is wrong with me? Why does he/she not feel the same? Can I do anything to change his/

her mind? Is it still possible for me to capture her heart? Can I remake myself to make me more attractive, appealing and thus loveable? Who will ever love me? Admittedly, these questions are really hard for someone who began asking them unconsciously as a helpless, sick and somewhat hopeless infant. "Will someone else love me unconditionally being that my biological parents were incapable of or unwilling to love me?"

I suspect you ask these questions in your own way. Freud suggests a full life consists of two main components: love and work.[3] Those two fundamental dimensions determine self-esteem. Does someone value me enough to accept me and love me regardless of my limitations, character defects and quirks? Will he or she look beyond my liabilities and willingly embrace a process of love which provides me with security and stability to achieve my potential and expand upon my internal assets? Each of us seeks at least one person who answers affirmatively "Yes" to those questions. Finding such a lover and beloved demonstrates self-worth to any person. With regard to work, each of us wants to feel a sense of accomplishment, success or excellence in a chosen field of labor and purpose. Whether a day laborer, janitor, sanitation employee, painter, electrician or a member of one of the learned professions, each of us aspires to achievement, promotion and praise. As we earn the respect of our coworkers and clients, we gain a greater sense of our self-worth. Beyond holding a job and proving we are employable, we need assurance that our hard work, knowledge and dedication possesses a determinative difference in the lives of the people whom we serve. Carl Jung discovered and defined the "mid-life crisis"[4] that afflicts everyone as he or she asks the question, "Does my work have any purpose other than a paycheck?" Have I contributed anything meaningful in my area of work? If not, then I need to make a fundamental change in order to fulfill a purpose other than earning my daily bread.

Nevertheless, uncertainty about love and work especially causes emotional and personal problems. Not knowing whether you are loved or not particularly obstructs your progress toward spiritual maturity and self-actualization. Repeated rejection, of your genuine love and willingness to learn how to love, by other people forces you to wonder whether you are loveable in the first place. How do you ride this emotional rollercoaster and heal from unrequited love and failed relationships?

Unrequited love influences self-perception and significantly hinders self-acceptance. Interestingly, in the emotional rubble of the damage and remains of failed relationships are the keys to healing, restoration and discovery of genuine love. Your perception of yourself seriously determines how other people view you. Notwithstanding the pitfalls of an inferiority complex that egotistical behavior veils, your projection of a healthy self-image, self-approval, self-love and self-acceptance usually draws similar types of people to you. They like what they see. They wish to warm by your internal fire. In time, they fall in love with your mind, heart, character and spirit as they realize that a long-term relationship with you means they will grow personally as the two of you commit to collective enlargement. Undoubtedly, the lack of self-acceptance repels people, and generally, persons who are on a path of spiritual and personal actualization. Such persons do not wish to save anyone or acquire any charity projects by way of a relationship. Loving someone who fails to accept himself or herself drains an emotionally healthy person of his or her own well-being. I have discovered that human beings cannot make another person whole. Only Almighty God can do so if He is sought. Accordingly, each instance of unrequited love and every failed relationship affords a person an opportunity to engage the arduous, bewildering, frightening, yet rewarding, process of self-discovery. How long, wide, deep, and high is your internal vacuum? Understanding that it is impossible to take another person hostage and coerce him or her to fill your internal space, how will you do so?

PUPPY LOVE

Unrequited love begins early in life and appears in many forms. Do you recall the first time you asked someone for a date and the person said "No?" As a grade school student, you gave extra candy on Valentine's Day to a classmate with the hopes that he/she would like you as much you liked him/her. You asked him/her for a chance to talk and he/she refused your advances. In high school, you really liked a classmate and thought you would be perfect together. You found the gumption to approach him/her. Startlingly, she thanks you for your kind feelings but tells you that he/she does not feel the same way about you. So, you end up at the prom with the person who will accompany you platonically; he/she too does not share any affectionate feelings for you though he/she respects your intellect and character. Your high school prom experience is a consolation prize rather than a first puppy love. As an adult, unrequited love manifests in many different and difficult types. Verbally and physically abusive relationships leave unhealed scars for decades. Relationships involving cohabiting often go awry. People invest time, money, sacrifices and their hearts expecting marriage only to discover that they have been "playing house" and simulating marriage with someone who never shared their commitment or dreams for a life together. Instead of purchasing an engagement ring to solidify the relationship, your partner signed a personal lease for another apartment. Often, broken engagements are more devastating than divorces. In the latter instance, you gave a marriage a fair try and it failed. In the former one, someone with whom you fell in love actually deprives you of the opportunity of demonstrating your ability and willingness to learn to love another person as you love yourself. Unknowingly, family and friends fuel feelings of inadequacy as they assume you are broken fundamentally; they reason your broken engagement obviously means you are too broken for marriage. If you falsely internalize those whispers and rumors, you fall prey to the scornful and sinful emotion, "I am unlovable." Broken engagements amongst other failed relationships culminate in self rejection. Unrequited love creates a victim's and rejection complex within a person's mind and heart.

> ## "Stop making people with present possibilities responsible for people with past problems."

NO ONE CAN HEAL YOU OTHER THAN YOURSELF

One of the worst strategies for healing from rejection in failed relationships is seeking someone to heal you. Naturally, you assume yet another person will cure your victim's complex. So, you look for someone who appears as needy as you are. Instead of entering a healthy relationship, you begin a symbiotic and hostage endeavor. A woman who failed to receive unconditional love from her father or a father figure in her childhood and adolescence inevitably looks for such qualities in another man. As she shares physical intimacy with him, she believes he unconditionally loves her. She forsakes the challenging emotional, mental and communication aspects of any good relationship. This man expects her to contribute as much in these areas as she does physically. Being a victim who suffers with rejection, and thereby expecting him to cure her pain, she searches for this type of man, whom she expects to give her the love she never had. She does not realize that there will never be a man who can fill the vacuum created by her father's absence. Ironically, she will reject eventually any man who attempts this mean feat. As she acquires a greater sense of self-acceptance and self-esteem, she resents her savior as he constantly reminds her of her past pain and brokenness. To avoid visiting her rejection upon another person, this woman must learn to process her own pain. Taking a hostage in a romantic relationship is not the answer. Talk openly, freely, straightforwardly and honestly with anyone with whom you relate romantically, sexually and emotionally. Grant them the dignity and respect to determine whether they willingly wish to support you as you heal and grow. Possibly, he or she can best assist your healing process as a friend instead of being a lover. Love freely and resist the temptation to take a hostage under the guise of loving someone with ulterior motives. I have dated people who were looking for love that they did not receive from their father, and I assure you, nothing is worse than trying to make up for a person who never existed. Little did I know, I was doing the same thing, trying to get people to make up for the absence of my biological parents, which was a task that was impossible.

One of the most damaging consequences of failed relationships and unrequited love is a person's tendency to internalize limiting beliefs. Someone tells you that you are not physically attractive. Another person demeans your background and education. Someone else emphasizes designer clothing and luxurious items; because you do not have them, they belittle you. Humorous comments and jokes laced with venom disguised in insults and condemnation. You are told that you are a nice person but it is so sad that you are poor. Though you are a hard worker with a very strong work ethic, someone concludes that you will not attain any economic or professional heights. Sharing a life with you means accepting a working class lifestyle. Pursuing genuine love, you undoubtedly have heard some form of these destructive words which wound deeply. The pain and scars last if you adopt these attitudes and beliefs. You cannot allow another person to define you. Criticism, however constructive, can only assist you as you mature spiritually and develop personally. When you accept negative and hurtful feedback from other people, you risk the danger of creating patterns in your consciousness, choices, and character. Though your ego instantaneously resists their remarks, you lapse inwardly into believing these people are correct. Those self-defacing and self-defeating attitudes significantly influence your behavior. You begin to project those estimations of you. You live according to the limits that you allow other people to put upon you. Hopelessly and helplessly accepting that you are incapable of exceeding the limitations that other people attempt to place upon you is the essence of limiting beliefs.

> *"Sometimes the people responsible for your pain are not the people around you, but it's sometimes the people inside of you who you have not released."*

FEAR WILL LIMIT YOU

As you may expect, fear factors significantly in cultivating limiting beliefs. As a consequence of a failed relationship, it is natural to fear that you will never find the right person and genuine love. You wonder whether you have been put on a treadmill of failed relationships. As they multiply, you may feel as if you are part of the wilderness wandering generation that completes the same circle for forty years before entering the Promised Land. Forsaking your obvious growth in any relationship, after a breakup, you may believe mistakenly that you are back at square one. That kind of erroneous thinking robs you of the emotional, mental and spiritual gains you have made through the relationships that did not endure. Additionally, fear magnifies the unfair and unreliable criticism of other people. Their false impressions of you begin to seem real and reliable. You begin to second guess yourself. You may spend ridiculous amounts of money and time on a wholesale self-improvement campaign. Surely, if you respond to their criticisms with making necessary adjustments to your physical appearance, physique, wardrobe and lifestyle, then the people who appeal to you must equally find you attractive. In many instances, you actually repel people as they relegate your self-improvement efforts as being shallow and insincere. Built upon fear and ego, a commercial and external makeover absolutely changes nothing in a person's character. Further, fear motivates you to run away from your internal challenges. "False Evidence Appearing Real" and "Forget Everything And Run," fear entices you to focus upon external circumstances rather than resolving your internal patterns that create resistance to your good and growth. Preoccupation with clothing, lifestyle, and outward appearances distract you from inner healing. It enables you to avoid painful feelings of rejection, betrayal, and abandonment. As a consequence, you still live with that pain and choose potential lovers and partners from the vantage point of that pain. You may also move geographically believing that a change in scenery and setting will alter fundamentally your chances of acquiring your heartfelt desire for genuine love. However, you will be the same person in each city. The emotional and personal liability of fear further entombs you to rejection from unrequited love and failed relationships. Insidiously, your fears deceive you into thinking that you are surmounting your pain and problems as you focus outwardly. Your distraction equates with delay of your healing from rejection. I pray you find God's grace and inner courage notwithstanding any angst and trepidation you may feel to confront and slay the Goliath of your fears.

FEAR WILL CREATE SELF-PITY

Fear usually creates the twin attributes of self-doubt and self-pity. Unknowingly, many victims of unrequited love and failed relationships become victimizers as they unconsciously want someone else to feel just as forcefully, the pain that they experienced. You would think that anyone on the receiving end of unrequited love would strive in every way to avoid inflicting that harsh pain upon another person. However, victims often utilize their self-doubt and self-pity as license to treat others any way they wish. This is what I did without thinking. I would make it my business to be the person who won whatever battle I thought I was fighting, not knowing that I was the only one in the ring swinging at a ghost, or maybe even my shadow trying to get a TKO on my feeling of rejection. After all, no one cared enough about me to spare my heart from breaking. Masked with bravado, victims retaliate against former lovers as they seek people to hurt as a means of catharsis. Being the object of someone else's affections and telling that person that you do not share his or her feelings seems empowering. As much as I did not enjoy breaking up whatever temporary romance I was involved with, it did made me feel wanted when the other person did not want to break-up. It's really sad when your self-worth is defined by letting go of someone who does not want to let go of you; and I had too many examples of this in my life that I wish I could take back. What I did learn over time is that I have choice and power as it relates to love. People will recover and move to another relationship just as I did.

FEAR LEADS TO WITHDRAWAL FROM OTHERS

Yet another means of expressing self-doubt and self-pity is withdrawal from the quest for intimacy and love. Under the guise of self-protection, you refuse blind dates, cancel plans, and avoid friends who are in relationships. Whereas your withdrawal lends itself to being a time of self-reflection, solitude and renewal, instead you may spend it licking your wounds and blaming others for your despair. Hoping to prevent ever feeling rejected and isolated again, you indirectly ensure your repetitive experience of those feelings as you nurse your resentments. *To resent means literally to relive*; practically speaking, feeling resentment equals replaying a frightening nightmare a thousand times. Nonetheless, perpetrating your pain upon a hapless and unsuspecting person is not a viable and lasting cure. In Tyler Perry's commercially successful movie, *The House That Preys*, Audrey Woodard's character, the wise and loving mother, rebukes her daughter, a character which Shania Latham plays, "Baby, don't you know that you can't make yourself happy by hurting other people." Likewise, you cannot heal by hurting someone else who seeks and shares your exact heartfelt desire for unconditional and genuine love. Additionally, isolation and abandoning a process of self-reflection and growth as you providentially and circumstantially await an introduction to the person with whom you will share love are not solutions. These differing kinds of self-doubt and self-pity further entomb you to a victim's mentality, rejection, fear and abandonment.

"What you fear the most is usually what is your biggest struggle."

In addition to isolationism, withdrawal and retaliation, the brutality of unrequited love and failed relationships hardens a pattern of insecurity in your thinking and creates defense mechanisms in your character. You live constantly on guard against pain of any type. Though you listen to the words and closely observe the actions of a potential mate, you do not trust him or her. Living with perpetual and pervasive fear of being hurt again, you wait for the next tragedy to befall you. Even when I found my wife and fell in love, there was still the feeling that she may reject me by calling off the engagement, wanting to return to her home city, or making a decision that would leave me alone without the love that I thought would be eternal. My wife one day told me as I was wandering in self-pity, "I was not the one who gave you up at birth, I am the one who accepted you and will be with you forever, so stop using your adoption as excuses for your immature behavior." As much as those words hit me to the core, they actually solidified what I was looking for, committed and eternal love. When you are fearful of rejection, you expect the absolute worse as you pretend and hope for the best. In "keeping it real," you plot an exit from a mushrooming relationship because you have a sixth sense that it will fail. To spare yourself the agony of yet another breakup, you end the relationship before it begins. You display arrogance, officiousness, impatience, intolerance and other offensive traits as a means of baiting the other person into leaving. Essentially, your deep-seated fears compel you to create a self-fulfilling anxiety, the dissolution of the relationship. Lying underneath your external behavior, your anger, resentment and thirst for revenge, having been a victim of unrequited love, motivates you to behave in this manner. These seductive emotions masquerade as empowering approaches to resolving our pain. On the contrary, they turn us into the biggest example of everything we despise as we become the victimizers that we swore we would never be. Accordingly, it is most important to live healthy through your experiences with unrequited love and failed relationships. Otherwise, your insecurity will prevent you from ever receiving new joys, mysteries and experiences of love. Most unfortunately, your low self-esteem coerces you to look for disappointment in every area of your life. These flawed and paralyzing emotions stunt your spiritual growth and personal actualization. Remarkably, they potentially create a monster within you who preys upon undeserving persons.

TRUE HEALING TAKES TIMES

Healing from rejection is not an easy or immediate process. It takes longer than reading this book. Hopefully, reading this book begins your process of healing and self-discovery. Even as I write these words and share my story, I progress in my healing process. I said it in the last paragraph, but I want to say it again to make sure that you get it. I recall using an excuse each time I did something wrong. I told my wife that my adoption explained my conduct as I still struggle with those issues. In time, my precious and loving wife replied, "Listen baby, I am not the one who gave you up for adoption. I refuse to accept your bitterness and crazy actions. I am here to support you through your ordeal but I am not here to be your emotional punching bag." I quickly changed my ways. That conversation with my wife taught me that I can control my emotions. Consider the fact that we rarely act out with authority figures such as police officers, principals and judges as we imagine the dreadful consequences. If we can redirect our frustrations in those situations, then we can behave similarly with people we love. Essentially, I encourage you to quit making excuses, as I did; and accept personal responsibility for your actions and life. As you realize that people and circumstances proverbially push your emotional buttons, assess your feelings and respond in the healthiest way. Each instance offers yet another chance to become a better person.

Unresolved issues relating to unrequited love and failed relationships potentially poison any future relationships. Seeing yourself as God sees you and learning unconditionally to accept and approve of yourself is the surest means to resurrection from rejection and abandonment by people whom you love but who do not feel similarly. Fascinatingly, gratitude ironically provides an additional means of healing from unrequited love. With time, patience and distance, you may discover with perfect hindsight that the relationship you deeply desired was not appropriate. Notwithstanding the pain you experienced in its aftermath, you would have felt limitless amounts of pain had you stayed in that relationship. Realizing God's kindness and grace in sparing you the debt, depression, disease, divorce, deceit and despair, that could have resulted, you offer genuine gratitude. As you do so, you heal from the pain you incurred and learn from the experience. Moreover, you forgive the person who hurt you. Forgiveness yields personal liberation regardless of how the person who harmed you responds. Not only do I forgive my biological parents for putting me up for adoption, I actually appreciate them. Their choice enabled me to be the recipient of my parents' genuine love. Perhaps, your experiences with unrequited love and failed relationships prepared you for the love of your life which you are better able to appreciate and nurture because of your past painful lessons. My biological parents were incapable of loving and rearing me as my parents did. With a deficiency in their characters or extremely limited financial, material, and educational resources, my biological parents would not have accomplished in my life what my parents did. Simply put, I am better off because I was not reared by them. I suspect you are better off because of your failed relationships. Sometimes you have to ask yourself, would your intended or desired person have valued you as you deserve? Be thankful for the dissolution of that relationship. Transform your rejection into motivation for success in love and work. Decide as you read these words to forgive anyone and everyone who has ever hurt you! Resolve, with God's help, to redeem your pain. Use it for a more productive purpose in your life than self-doubt and self-pity. Summarily, self-approval, self-acceptance, forgiveness and gratitude are daily and practical means of rebirth and recovery in response to unrequited love and failed relationships.

"Healing is not a weekend course, but it is a lifetimes of working on yourself week after week until you have become victorious over your challenges."

YOU CAN RISE ABOVE YOUR FEARS

Incredibly, you can fall in love despite rejection from previous love interests. Resolving rejection issues opens the door to genuine love. The furnace of affliction often burns away dross in a person's character. Just as a refiner leaves gold, silver and other precious metals in a fiercely burning oven to allow the hot temperatures to remove impurities, life often utilizes unrequited love and failed relationships to accomplish a parallel purpose in us. Otherwise, we would not know what genuine, honest, respectful, selfless, and sacrificial love is. We would use textbooks to theorize about love. As we learn from past mistakes, we are most capable of giving and receiving love. The primary step, however, is learning to love and accept yourself as God does (Psalm 139:13-16). A healthy sense of self allows you to be vulnerable to another person. You become willing to try openly and freely to experience love. Given your expensive lessons from the past, you can trust yourself; you will not permit an insincere person to waste your time and squander your emotions as you will be able quickly to detect their ulterior motives. Still, you maintain your personal process of healing to ensure you contribute daily and constantly to a healthy and growing relationship. I am thankful to God for sending me Danielle who loves me unconditionally, and who has made the commitment of growing with me through various challenges. The power of God is that He knows who you need. I remember praying when I was seeking a wife after being tired of the single life. My prayer went just like this, "God, I am ready to be married, please send me who I need, but make me want them." I was tired of just going after relationships for the sake of temporary companionship; I was ready to experience real love. However, because I was scared of rejection, I had to ask the Lord to work on me and send me the person who would love me unconditionally as He continued working on me. I can honestly say, the Lord answered my prayers. Guess what? God is not selfish. He can also do the same for you; you just have to believe and trust Him. It may not be a romantic spouse that you are in need of right now. You may be in need of a friend or a mentor who you can open your heart up to. Like Proverbs 18:24 says, ask God to help you to become friendly as you are looking for someone to be friendly towards you. If you pray and believe, I am sure that in time, your prayer request will be answered. People often tell me, "You seem so happy now." My only response is, "I am because I have the person who was sent by God to me." People also ask me, "How are you enjoying marriage life?" I quickly respond by saying, "Marriage life is awesome, but the person I married is outstanding." I encourage you to make sure you pray about the people you bring into your life. The prayer I always encourage people to say is very simple, it goes like this: "*God, whoever is in my life that you did not place, please remove; and whoever is not in my life that you desire, please reveal them to me and replace them for me. In Jesus name, Amen!*"

"The word 'Romance', according to the dictionary, means excitement, adventure, and something extremely real. Romance should last a lifetime." —Billy Graham[5]

5 TYPES OF RELATIONSHIPS TO AVOID

1. Avoid one-sided beneficial relationships.

2. Avoid rebound relationships.

3. Avoid symbiotic relationships in which two very needy people attempt to fill each other's void.

4. Avoid emotionally, verbally and physically abusive relationships.

5. Avoid superficial relationships built mostly upon external factors such as money, education, social class, physical attractiveness, etc.

Additionally, I offer several helpful hints in discovering and actualizing healthy and loving relationships:

- Read the story of The Three Princes of Serendip who stumble upon their destiny en route to something else.
- Your ideal loving relationship may emerge serendipitously.
- Relationships are ironic. When you look for them, you rarely find them; when you cease looking, they mystically appear.
- Consider the role of divine orchestration in discovering and actualizing healthy and loving relationships.
- Ask Almighty God for discernment, knowledge and wisdom in choosing a mate.
- Do not expect from a mate anything you are unwilling to give.
- Choose a friend with whom you can grow.
- Wisely and willingly share your past pain and personal story of healing.
- Make a thorough internal inventory of your assets and liabilities.
- As it relates to marriage, clarify your non-negotiable requirements for the relationship; it stands to reason that you would ask your prospective mate to do the same.

10 QUESTIONS TO ASK YOURSELF ABOUT REJECTION: BE HONEST IN YOUR ANSWERS

1. When people act like you are not good enough for them, do you chase them, and try to prove yourself to them?

2. When you get rejected do you think that something is wrong with you?

3. Have you ever tried to make someone who doesn't like you like you?

4. Do you have a bad habit of constantly worrying about what others think of you?

5. Do you ever fear of failing in front of someone, so as a result, you never try anything you are not 100% sure you can succeed at?

6. Are you afraid to be honest with someone because you fear it may end the friendship or relationship?

7. Have you given up on some goals in your life as a result of someone you trust not believing in your goal or desire?

8. Have you ever failed at something and are afraid to try again?

9. Have you seen so many UNHEALTHY relationships that you have begun to believe that there is no such thing as a HEALTHY relationship?

10. Have you ever prayed about your fears and truly left them in the hands of the Lord?

REVIEW QUESTIONS

When it comes to your emotions, how do you normally act?

☐ Very Expressive

☐ Extremely Private

☐ Expressive & Private

Has the feeling of rejection ever kept you from being able to give and/or receive love?

☐ I have never allowed myself to be in-love

☐ I have never allowed myself to receive love

☐ I am good at receiving, but not good at giving

☐ I am good at giving, but not good at receiving

Growing up as a child, did you see love in your home?

☐ Yes

☐ No

☐ Sometimes

☐ I can't remember

Do you love yourself?

☐ I do love myself

☐ I don't love myself

☐ Sometimes

☐ No

Are you honest with yourself about your limitations, mistakes or short-comings?

☐ It's hard for me to tell myself the truth about me

☐ I am scared to really look inside and see who I am

☐ I am always honest with myself about my reality

☐ I usually only admit my short-comings when I am forced to face them

Has fear ever kept you from pursuing a goal or dream?

☐ Yes

☐ No

If you answered YES to the previous questions, write down some dreams and goals and make it your business to pursue them at all cost.

_____

_____

_____

When a relationship is over or a friendship ends, how do you normally act?

☐ Like I don't care

☐ Seek to understand why

☐ I act like I don't care just to save face

☐ It all depends on the relationship

ENDNOTES

1   Wilde, Oscar. http://www.brainyquote.com/quotes/quotes/o/oscarwilde103614.html

2   Tennyson, Alfred Lord. http://www.brainyquote.com/quotes/quotes/a/alfredlord153702.html

3   Freud, Sigmund. http://www.brainyquote.com/quotes/authors/s/sigmund_freud.html

4   Jung, Carl Gustav. As discussed in Murray Stein, *In Midlife: A Jungian Perspective* (Woodstock, CT: Spring Publications, Inc., 1983).

5   Graham, Billy. http://www.brainyquote.com/quotes/quotes/b/billygraha394202.html

HEALING 5
YOU ARE ABLE TO IMPROVE: HEALING FROM TERMINATION

"In great times of stress or adversity, it's always best to keep busy, to plow your anger and your energy into something positive." —Lee Iacocca[1]

A colleague recently shared a story of termination with me. He learned of a church in Harlem where a new pastor insisted all employees had to have a college degree. This pastor summarily dismissed anyone who did not have a bachelor's degree or higher. He reasoned this requirement ensures the congregation receives quality from its staff and other employees. As would be the case normally, the sexton did not have a college degree. Accordingly, he lost his job. As this janitor left the church on that fateful day, he pondered the unjustness of the pastor's decision to terminate his employment. Simply, the policy seemed unfair, unprincipled and unreasonable. However, as this terminated janitor took that long stroll home to tell his wife that he would be pounding the pavement looking for a job, he closely observed his surroundings. As he looked deeply into the setting and actions of the people he passed within his two mile walk, he stumbled upon an idea that would change his life and fortunes. Ironically, he realized that his unjust termination would become the catalyst of divine favor and grace in his life. Unbeknownst to him at the time, the janitor eventually appreciated the pastor's decision as it forced the janitor onto the path of his destiny. The darkness that covered his thoughts and feelings on the afternoon he learned he lost job, in time, yielded clarity that enabled him to achieve his destiny.

Termination from an unfulfilling job whether you are underemployed or undercompensated could be the means of resurrection from the lingering death of a dead-end job. Still, it hurts when you are fired unjustly from a job where you performed diligently, professionally and faithfully. Understandably, you feel victimized when you realize the persons with whom you worked never really appreciated you or your contributions. Arriving an hour or more before everyone else in the mornings and staying late practically each evening, you went above and beyond the specific items of your job description. You even worked weekends to assist with projects to prevent your division from falling behind. Rarely, you denied requests to help other employees and needy clients. Nevertheless, jealousy, miscommunication, indifference and personality clashes conspired to affect your wrongful termination. Not surprisingly, as you physically leave your previous place of employment, you depart with a boat load of feelings mostly summed up in one word, rejection.

For many people, the relationships within the work environment parallel their families of origin and formative years. Unconsciously, they live within the complexity and confusion of the difficult emotions and feelings of early childhood and adolescence. They respond to people as if they were unloving parents, spiteful siblings, and annoying cousins. In compliments, they hear the cloying and sentimental words of a doting grandmother. When someone offers constructive criticism, they hear the harsh rebuke of an overbearing and insensitive grandfather. If a coworker fails to pull his or her weight and these people have to compensate, the experience jettisons back to a shared bedroom in which a sibling again failed to clean his or her side of the room. Unaware of this tendency, sometimes people assign coworkers to the roles that their parents and siblings had in their families of origin. As a consequence, they expect the people with whom they work to interact with them in the same way that their relatives do. Further, termination equates with being kicked out of the family instead of dismissed from a place of employment. Come on, you know I am talking REAL. Have you ever felt like this?

Ok, allow me to push my claim. People have the tendency to transform the work environment into family. Primary feelings of anger, bitterness, fear, depression and resentment would compound an experience with termination. However justified, legal, necessary, or even providential, termination feels as if it was a betrayal. People whom you trusted conspired to deprive you of your ability to earn your daily bread and provide for your family. In short, they banded together to reject you. This is simply saying that people who often feel rejected carry that same feeling to their jobs, and when their ideas or opinions are not accepted, they interpret that as continued rejection in their lives. If you are going to be successful in your profession, you cannot allow the bitter pain of internal rejection from your past to leak its way into your career. I've seen many people miss promotions and great careers all because they did not know how to deal with personal issues in their public life. Do not allow this to be your story.

"Never allow your internal pain to cause you to interrupt your financial gain. When your worries become obstacles for your work, you run the risk of losing what you can gain, because you never let go of what you have."

SEPARATING EMOTIONS FROM EMPLOYMENT

One of the first steps in healing from termination and the feelings of rejection that accompany this hard experience is distinguishing the work environment from your nuclear family. Release your expectations of coworkers to care for you as your family did and does. Actually, learn to release other people's opinions and expectations of you. A friend of mine offers some very helpful advice, **"Other people's opinions of you are not your business. Learn to mind your own business."** The people with whom you work are under no obligation to nurture you as your parents and siblings would. Your relationships in the workplace are strictly professional. Whereas, friendships and loyalties may result in time, it is improper to assume that your coworkers owe you anything other than the requisite respect and ethics of a professional relationship. Maintaining a proper emotional perspective of workplace relationships prevents slippage into the quicksand of betrayal and rejection. Should you be drowning in a cesspool of such thoughts and feelings, resist the temptation to sink deeper by nursing imaginations of enacting revenge. Instead, I suggest you straightforwardly accept the nature of work relationships and release your unrealistic expectations.

Undoubtedly, darkness surrounds termination. Depression can naturally emerge as you begin to blame yourself and you wonder why you failed to see the deception beforehand. Fear increases as you think about your familial and financial obligations. The frightening job market with so few prospects and positions for so many qualified people makes you feel helpless and powerless. What will you do? Hopelessness magnifies in your thoughts as you bewilderingly glare at a very bleak future. Possibly, you digress to your primal fears in childhood. If you were unable to depend upon your parents and other adults to care responsibly for you during your formative years, you certainly felt as though they abandoned and neglected you. You felt as if you were made to become an adult at a very early age. Perhaps, you started doing your own laundry at eight years old because you were tired of being overlooked on wash day in your family. Maybe, your dependable and faithful work ethic originated in your being tired of wearing hand-me-down clothes. Your summer time shorts were the long pants of the winter that were now too short. Frustrated with that situation and deeply desiring new clothes, you grabbed the lawnmower and began to mow neighbor's yards to earn money. After you saved enough, you took the bus into town and bought yourself some brand new cool clothes. These memories simultaneously encourage and depress you. Rightly, you still feel a lot of pride about becoming increasingly independent in your adolescence. However, you mourn the loss of your childhood years when you should have been allowed to stumble and fall as you grew up. Therefore, years later, these experiences, coupled with termination from a job, can pull you back into the emotional muck and mire of feeling abandoned and rejected. It is as if your bosses assumed the role of your parents and other adults who failed you. Resentment mounts as you relive those childhood fears. So many negative emotions rise and form a deep dark cloud over your consciousness and character.

ONE DOOR CLOSED, ANOTHER DOOR OPENS

Interestingly, the darkness of termination opens the door to personal destiny. One of the surest ways of experiencing resurrection from this type of rejection is accepting that it may be one of the best occurrences in your life. Termination causes desperation which in turn coerces creativity. A person hardly examines his life and opportunities when he rests happy and content on any job, particularly a good paying job that demands little in terms in of productivity and imagination. Yet, the discomfort of termination forces a person to pause and ponder his life, specifically his employment. Admittedly, you need periods of time to adjust emotionally to termination if you mainly feel you were let go unjustly. The pendulum of anger and depression must swing back and forth until it rests. Before you begin a job search, you assess the Pandora's Box of emotions emanating from your warrantless firing. Were lesser talented and committed people allowed to remain? Was your job eliminated to save someone who was romantically involved with one of the decision makers? Was your salary divided to give raises to other people who were not as productive? Were you fired simply because your boss did not like you and could terminate the position with impunity? An inexhaustible list of such questions spontaneously pops up in your thoughts. Inevitably, anger yields to sadness and pity as you begin a job search with few prospects. Rather than being a sign of weakness, your sadness can be a turning point. With the humility, meekness, and graciousness that sadness and limitations often produce, genuinely ask Almighty God for guidance and clarity as you embrace this process of personal growth as it motivates you to examine your life and use of your time and talents.

> "A door closed in one area may mean that a larger door
> is open in another area, which one will you focus on,
> the closed door, or the possible open door?"

Are you living the life you imagined? Answer in one word. If not, what prevents you from doing so? Are you frightened to risk the resources and time to pursue your dream job or business? Are you afraid to invest in yourself? Have you utilized the last five years as wisely as possible? In the next five years, will you have a job or will you have a career? Do you awake each morning to go to a job or purpose? Have any of your jobs had a purpose other than earning your daily bread and meeting your financial obligations? Have you achieved any depth of proficiency and productivity in your profession? The circumstances of living between jobs thrust these questions upon a person. Learning to be quiet, sit still, stand aside, cease busyness, and listen for answers is worthwhile before launching yet another job search. A period of unemployment is a good time to draft, define, or refine a personal mission statement. Perhaps, in the dark sky of termination and indecision, you can see the stars of youthful dreams more clearly than ever.

TURNING YOUR TERMINATION INTO YOUR ELEVATION

How do you turn a termination into an asset? Search the rubble for hidden riches and lessons. Mysteriously, God utilizes endings as new beginnings. As the title of a bestselling Christian growth book, *Necessary Endings*[2], reflects, there are times in life when some doors must close completely and irreversibly to enable other doors to open. Some people will not find genuine love until they close the door of past flames and affairs in their hearts. As long as they look backwards, they remain blind to the brightness of new beginnings. Jesus says anyone who puts his hands on the gospel plow and looks back to the world is not fit for service in the kingdom of God. Double-mindedness rarely accomplishes anything; it furthers confusion and ineffectiveness. Often, success and excellence in any field or trade require single-minded focus and tunnel vision commitment. In order to achieve this type of dedication, a person must cut ties with unnecessary distractions. **A first step in transforming a termination from being a liability into an asset is conducting a post mortem**

examination. What fundamentally caused the termination? What can you learn? How do you grow from the experience? What do you need to know about yourself as you pursue other opportunities? What are your strengths and weaknesses? How can you enhance your strengths? How can you neutralize your weaknesses? What do you care to do to make a living? How can you live the life you imagine? **Second, look for ways to correct your previous mistakes.** Did you allow small and simple yet significant tasks such as punctuality, attendance, typographical errors, timely follow-up, and attention to detail to undermine the quality of your work? Did you build strategic, mutually respectful, and lasting collegial relationships? After all, much of human progress depends greatly on and occurs largely because of honest, forthright, and fruitful relationships. Self-evaluation and persistently examining daily experiences combine to change life's obstacles into opportunities. Those two cardinal spiritual disciplines are the best means of turning a termination into an asset

How does termination assist you in progressing toward your destiny? While seeking employment, it is helpful to drill deeply within self-analysis and professional assessment. Take a comprehensive inventory of yourself. Today, we have the advantage of numerous social scientific and methodologically respectable tests which correctly encourage and empower you in determining the most compatible professions and jobs for your personality and skills. I suggest Meyers-Briggs[3], Enneagram's Strength Finder[4], and Authentic Happiness[5] are reliable and helpful tools to assist you in progressing toward your career and destiny. Among many other options, these tests are available online at reasonable cost. Second, consider personal and vocational counseling. Sometimes, this confidential and professional interaction helps crystallize your intuition and hunches about how you wish to spend your working years. Psychotherapy offers a safe space to unearth the layers of feelings and experiences that contribute to internal dynamics that unconsciously undermine your good and growth. Beyond a formal vocational analysis, a life coach is someone who professionally parallels a physical trainer. They will walk beside you as you embark upon a new phase of employment and life. They will assist you in maintaining rigid honesty and discipline as you boldly strive to actualize the dreams of your youth and live the life you imagined. As an accountability partner, a life coach excels in facilitating a constant conversation with your innermost self. Daily prayer, meditation, and study of scriptures open the eyes of your mind and heart, thereby enabling you to view your life in small and large detail. Spiritual disciplines focus upon specific trees in the forest but also provide a panoramic view. These spiritual practices reveal your mission and purpose while also discerning practical and pragmatic ways of accomplishing them. A season of unemployment affords you the time and ability to compose a pragmatic and practical mission statement for your current season of life. As a consequence, you maximize your current opportunities without losing focus of a larger, overarching purpose of acquiring "true ambition," which one author defines as "the deep desire to live usefully and walk humbly under the grace of God." Were you to utilize this period of termination for self-analysis and professional evaluation, undoubtedly, you would have devised and pursued a plan for your next position as it accords with your mission and purpose. Strangely, it requires the time and solitude that termination often creates to motivate most people to commit to this important personal and professional task.

"Just because you have been fired from your job, that doesn't mean that you were fired from your purpose. Don't confuse what you do temporarily with what you were called to do eternally."

Obvious similarities exist between employing the foregoing strategies for resolving termination by seeking and finding a new job with healing from any type of rejection. As you dissect an occurrence of termination to determine its root causes, equally, you dissect any feelings of rejection you experience. What are your true base and elementary feelings and thoughts? Forsake the tendency to rely upon anger, resentment, and bitterness because those volcanic emotions appear more empowering than more authentic emotions of sadness, depression, bewilderment, and grief. How does your experience with rejection really make you feel? Consider following Celie's example in Alice Walker's Pulitzer Prize winning and internationally bestselling book, *The Color Purple*, of writing frank letters to God and expressing your raw feelings. Like hot lava erupting from an active volcano, anger and its companion emotions are destructive. Pain which touches a beating heart redeems suffering more quickly than righteous indignation achieves justice. In essence, when the pains of life connect with your heart that seeks to live, you are able to fight the pain that wants you to give up, and pull your strength from your heart that wants you to live in spite of the pain. Resolving pain and its accompanying feelings of victimization, low self-esteem, and abandonment transforms hurtful experiences into attributes of strengths. Unresolved disputes whether legal or romantic, potentially yield bitterness as it is difficult to forgive and release anger when you feel as if someone who harmed you evaded justice. Still, a primary step in healing from rejection of any type is honestly and directly embracing your feelings.

Systems organizers define "Total Quality Management,"[6] as the strategy of examining each small detail to assess its influence upon a department's productivity. They use the fishbone as an association and means of meticulously dissecting minute events and emotions. Similarly, you might draw a fishbone and detail your feelings to determine the deepest and most prevailing ones. Humbly and genuinely ask for God's help in the process of healing. Utilize self-assessment tools to evaluate patterns in your thoughts, actions and personality that perpetuate them. Are you easily seduced by melodrama and sentimentality? Do you feel more alive in the midst of chaos? Knowledge of any patterns is the first step in breaking them. Practically, counseling and a life coach will assist in resolving your intrapersonal and interpersonal dilemmas just as they would in helping you to evade assuming another dead-end and unfulfilling job. Yet again, the daily practice of different spiritual disciplines will sustain you as your journey toward inner healing and wholeness. Chiefly, prayer, meditation, study of scriptures, and commitment to strengthening a relationship with Almighty God are the surest means of actualizing divine assistance in healing from rejection and abandonment. The Psalter offers enduring encouragement. "Though my mother and father forsake me, the Lord will receive me," (Psalm 27:10). Consistent communion with God utilizing these spiritual graces certainly clarifies your mission and purpose. Eventually, you discover your earthly purpose and its eternal value.

REINVENT YOURSELF FOR YOUR FUTURE

Essentially, healing from rejection borne of termination emerges when you use the time to redefine your mission and purpose. Do not allow your feelings to hinder your progress toward a more meaningful job. Take the time to process your feelings. Dig deeply to unearth the core feelings that obstruct your good and growth. Allow yourself to authentically feel your pain rather than use anger and other toxic emotions to compel you to act contrary to your true feelings. As your Heavenly Father, God expects to hear your real and honest pain. Like any good parent, He waits to comfort you and share His love and encouragement with you. Your continual communion with your Heavenly Father will transform your pain into purpose. As you live within your specific purpose, you experience healing from any type of rejection. In short, He resurrects you to new life.

LIGHTS OUT BECOMES LIGHTS ON

My wife, Danielle, was living a good life as she was receiving income from her job and support from her loving father. As fate would have it, she lost her job and was scared of how she would make it. In addition to all of this, her only reliable car was in the repair shop. However, she knew she could not tell her father that she was unemployed because he would make the suggestion of returning home to Lake Charles, which she did not want to do. House lights were turned off, money was drying up, and she did not know how she was going to make it. One day, prior to this, she told her father, "Dad, it's time that you allow me to grow up and become the woman that you and momma raised me to be." This was a tough decision for her, but she made this decision. As she journeyed through this process of living without lights, depending on people and public transportation to get from one location to the next, she inevitably grew in her dependence upon her Heavenly Father more than her earthly father. To make a long story short, her termination from her job allowed her to grow up into a woman whose faith became more important than her finances. God provided everything she needed. As time passed, she was looking for another job. She completed an online employment search and submitted her resume. Contrary to what she was taught in business school, before pressing send, she made the decision to list that she was a Christian woman. When her now mentor, J. Otis Mitchell, owner of a prominent CPA Firm in Houston, Texas, was looking at her application, although her experience was not to the level of his desire, he saw that she was a Christian and decided to give her a chance on that basis. As fate would have it, that chance led her to begin a career that opened the door to many blessings. She went from being an inexperienced Accountant to a well-rounded and knowledgeable Accountant with skills that only few have. To make the story even sweeter, it led her to serve in a position as Senior Accountant of a ministry where she manages millions of dollars. In addition to this, as a result of her profession and position, I was present when she came to her boss' office, Reverend Terrance Johnson, who is a close friend of mine. This encounter established a friendship, which led to dating, which led to our marriage. However, when she was going through the dark stages of her life, if she had taken the easy way out and depended on her father to provide her needs, she ultimately would have never been in a place that led to her meeting the one she would marry. She did not know at the time that God was ordering her steps. The reason why many of us miss our blessings is because we seek to take the easy way out. I say this to emphasize that when you are released from a job, do not get upset with the employer. Trust that God is behind the scene working on your future in ways that you will never imagine. Therefore, I thank God that she lost her job, because losing her job allowed me to find my partner who has become my help-meet.

"Light is most appreciated in dark places.
Never despise your dark places. . .crevices, closets
and caves are where you experience your greatest light."

THANK YOU FOR FIRING ME

Let me close by returning to the opening story. What became of the janitor whom the pastor unjustly and misguidedly fired? As he walked home that fateful and awful day, he noticed numerous people who were smoking. However, he did not see any bodegas or kiosks where these countless smokers could purchase cigarettes and other tobacco products. All of those smokers had to travel a mile or more to purchase any "smokes." In due time, this man made his first investment in a cigarette, newspaper, candy, and beverage stand. He expanded upon his instantaneous success by acquiring several additional kiosks. Eventually, this savvy businessman who discovered his acumen, within the darkness of termination, became a millionaire and won accolades and admiration of many persons in the business community. In an interview, someone asked him to imagine what he would have accomplished had he gone to college. He responded, "I would have been a janitor with a college degree."

> *"Let me embrace thee, sour adversity, for wise men say it is the best course."*
> *—William Shakespeare*

5 HELPFUL HINTS FOR RESOLVING TERMINATION

1. Do not internalize the incident.

2. Do not uncritically accept destructive criticism.

3. Commit to learning from the experience: what lessons do you take away from the experience.

4. Forgive the people who treated you unfairly and jeopardized your life and the well-being of your family.

5. Learn to relinquish your intense emotions about the experience.

5 HELPFUL HINTS IN PROGRESSING BEYOND TERMINATION

1. Resolve to capitalize upon termination.

2. Embrace the darkness of termination.

3. Do not allow the darkness before the dawn to paralyze you. Resurrection occurs "while it is still dark" and "just before sunrise."

4. Transform your termination into an asset.

5. Persevere through the darkness of termination toward the light of your destiny.

REVIEW QUESTIONS

Right now, are you doing what you planned to do in life with your career?

☐ Yes

☐ No

☐ Unemployed

Are you happy with your present profession/career?

☐ Yes

☐ Sometimes

☐ No

How well do you interact with people?

☐ I am a loner.

☐ I normally wait for people to interact with me.

☐ I take initiative in interacting with people.

☐ I am terrible when it comes to my interpersonal skills.

How do you handle bad experiences or days on your job?

☐ I take the frustration home and dump it on my family.

☐ I leave work problems on the job.

☐ I allow it to build up inside of me and cause me stress.

☐ I do not take anything personally that happens at work.

☐ Other: _____

_____

_____

Do you tend to look for the "good" in "bad" situations?

☐ Yes because I am a positive person.

☐ No, it is what it is, I am a realist.

What do you do to improve yourself as a person who has a desire for greater success?

☐ Study the field that I am in.

☐ Look for people to mentor me.

☐ Ask questions from those around me.

☐ Attend conferences, etc.

☐ Other: _____

_____

_____

Have you ever had an experience that you did not appreciate at the time but you have since come to realize that it has made you a better person? If YES, write down what that experience was.

☐ Yes _____

_____

_____

☐ No

ENDNOTES

1   Iacocca, Lee. http://www.brainyquote.com/quotes/quotes/l/leeiacocca138442.html

2   Cloud, Henry. *Necessary Endings: The Employees, Businesses and Relationships That All of Us Have to Give Up to Move Forward* (San Francisco: Harper Business, 2011)

3   The Meyers and Briggs Foundation. http://www.myersbriggs.org/my-mbti-personality-type/mbti-basics/

4   The Enneagram Institute. http://www.enneagraminstitute.com/

5   Seligman, Martin E. P. *Authentic Happiness: Using the New Positive Psychology to Realize Your Potential for Lasting Fulfillment* (New York: Free Press, 2002)

6   American Society for Quality. "Total Quality Management," http://asq.org/learn-about-quality/total-quality-management/overview/overview.html

HEALING 6
YOU ARE LOVED UNCONDITIONALLY: HEALING FROM FEELING REJECTED BY GOD

"I believe that unarmed truth and unconditional love will have the last word."

—Martin Luther King, Jr.[1]

WHAT ARE YOU THINKING?

How should I begin this chapter? I know…I am going to make you think for a second. Let's go! Pause for a moment and consider whether you have ever been happy, joyous, and free in your life. Have you? If not, what explains your inability to experience the life you imagine? As one healing from abandonment and rejection, I suspect you have lived with an ever burning flame of sadness and depression. Self-pity – low self-esteem – loneliness – isolation – poverty – hopelessness – unrequited love – multiple and different failures – emotional disappointments – bewilderment. Hardly a complete list, these feelings describe just how gloomy and lonely the world is for you. In the midst of crowds, whether a crowded airport or a large holiday gathering of family members, you feel very alone. Does anyone care? To avoid these raw and real emotions of depression and desolation, you possibly built a public persona fueled by anger, bitterness, strife, resentment, vengeance, and venom. These feelings seductively appear more empowering than unhappiness and fear. For nearly a quarter of a century, I fell for the misleading notion that anger and its many offshoots would empower me to overcome my feelings of abandonment and rejection. Like hot lava spewing from an active volcano, my anger destroyed anything in its path. It actually reinforced my sadness and loneliness as it eliminated all relationships and ruined job opportunities. Very few people have time, willingness and graciousness to assist an angry person in healing from the underlying causes of his fury. Most people decide to relate and work with people who are not angry. Nonetheless, I speculate that a deep feeling that even Almighty God has rejected you lies beneath your lifelong despair. *Depression is anger turned inward.* After the flames and fumes of your anger dissipate, you crash emotionally and are left with your authentic and lasting feelings of sadness and depression. As you no longer fight these attitudes, you face the hard reality that you remain in a wilderness where you constantly feel anguish and misery as you strive for freedom, joy, and happiness. Simultaneously, you wrestle with these deep-seated feelings and wonder why God allows such gloominess in your life.

Why does God allow so much pain and suffering in my life? What have I done to deserve the rejection and its residual affects and effects upon my life? These personal questions are practical versions of the enduring theological problem of evil. For centuries, theologians and philosophers continue to debate and analyze the existence of an all-powerful, all-knowing, ever-present and all-kind God, and prevalent evil in the world. Is God not powerful enough to defeat evil? With perfect foreknowledge, God can prevent evil. If He is everywhere, how does He observe and permit evil deeds? Is He truly all-kind if He fails to intervene in human affairs and ensure justice in response to human evil? Should you ask any of these formal academic questions, I mostly refer you to the works of Augustine, Aquinas, the Church Fathers, and numerous other systematic theologians whose answers remain relevant in the twenty-first century.

For a more practical and pragmatic treatment of the subject, I suggest two books. First, John Swinton argues in his compelling book, *Raging with Compassion: Pastoral Responses to the Problem of Evil*[2], that congregations are ideal settings for victims of evil as collective Christian communities provide love, comfort, care and advocacy for brothers and sisters who experience tragedy. Second, Rabbi Harold Kushner's enduring bestseller, *When Bad Things Happen to Good People*[3], offers very personally applicable solutions as people within all types of faith communities struggle to heal from evil. More personally, in keeping with the theme of this book, I translate this major theological problem into a basic question. Has God also rejected and abandoned me? If not, how do I heal from feeling that He has? Essentially, all types of rejection cumulate in this question. Whether it is abandonment by biological parents, denial of adoptive parents, myriad experiences with unrequited love and failed relationships, termination from employment, you somehow feel that God deserted you as He allowed these misfortunes. Why does He not give you advance warning of approaching danger? Should not God reveal to you the best choices in any situation? Is it not sadistic of God to stand by idly and watch you travel in the direction of a storm? Feeling rejected by people is one thing; however, feeling that God, your Heavenly Father, rejects you is quite another. As I staggered forward through the maze and haze of abandonment, anger, and rejection, I often asked, "If God loved me unconditionally, why did He allow me to be born sick and why did He allow my parents to abandon me?"

"If God brings you to it, He will bring you through it."

Perhaps, you are dealing with issues in your life that leave you with the feeling God does not love you. There are times when your circumstances eclipse God's presence and unfailing love. Repeated failures in love and work generally result in sadness and depression for which you usually blame God as His love, guidance, and protection should combine to prevent these occurrences. After a while, you question the worth of prayer and other spiritual disciplines. Certainly, it is difficult to feel as if you are a recipient of God's amazing grace. The constant recitation of Bible verses such as, "The Lord will never leave thee nor forsake thee," hardly penetrates the citadel of cynicism you build mentally and emotionally. Having lived within such a fortress of fear for many years, I am well acquainted with conflicting emotions convincing me that even Almighty God Himself abandons me! However, as I live through the dark night of the soul when darkness is deepest, early morning winds are coldest, and minute sounds magnify into frightening feelings, I equally know the promise and power of persevering toward the dawn. In a conversation with Dr. Ralph West, affectionately known as "Poppa West," I learned how to transfer my feelings about divine abandonment into a new realization of God's genuinely unfailing love. As an adopted child, I assumed that God participated in and sanctioned my biological parents' decision to abandon me. I did not appreciate that God was in the room as they made a very human, and perhaps reasonable, decision at that juncture in their lives and personal development. In His perfect foreknowledge and infinite wisdom, Almighty God prepared for that moment by placing His love in the minds and hearts of my adoptive parents. He blessed me with parents who would love me more than I could ever desire. In addition, I now wonder whether my biological parents offered a prayer as they made that fateful choice. Possibly, they prayed, "Lord, we are unable to care for this child; please place him in the hands of someone who can love him and rear him to serve you." "Poppa West's" sage perspective gave me a whole new outlook upon God's love. Instead of abandoning me, God, "the Giver of every good and perfect gift," demonstrated His unfailing love in the persons, selflessness, sacrifices, and redemption of my adoptive parents.

THE PRODIGAL SON

As I think about my longstanding feelings that perhaps even God abandoned me, I again recall the story of the prodigal son. This younger son demanded his inheritance from his loving father years before the son was entitled legally to receive it. Rebellious and impulsive, this son liquated his assets and set off to a foreign land to engage in riotous living. Immature, arrogant and indifferent, this son assumes he knows more than his father. He self-righteously tramples upon his father's indescribable love. As I apply this well-known biblical story, I accept that my complaints and anger equated with indicting God for failing to help me at my most vulnerable moment. My rage and resentment about my abandonment and adoption equaled a decision to take my life into my own hands. Like the prodigal son, I left my home after high school and sought to design my own life according to my personal desires and whims. As the story of the prodigal son unfolds, he ends up in a pig pen feeding swine. In the phraseology of the American South, the prodigal son was "slopping the hogs" for a living. He poured the "slop" (a bucket full of dirty dish water, rotten food, bones, scraps, molded bread and anything else discarded from the kitchen) into troughs hoping to escape wallowing pigs as they violently shook their urine and feces infested mud. Nonetheless, he comes to his senses and remembers his father's unfailing love. The prodigal arises from his destitution and returns to his father's home where the son receives a welcome of unconditional love. As I descended to the uttermost depths of sadness, depression and darkness, I, like the prodigal son, came to my senses. I acknowledged that God loves me with an unfailing love which transcends any circumstance. I discard any notion that He forsakes or leaves me as I grow in relationship with Him. I trust God and His faithfulness. One of my favorite Bible verses, Psalm 27:10, says, "If my mother and father forsake me, the Lord will receive me." Some translations of that verse state "the Lord will take me up." In that neonatal unit, the Lord lifted me from the mire of abandonment and put me in the arms of loving parents. My moment of truth came as I talked with Dr. West and other persons whom God utilized to open the eyes of my mind and heart. I, too, returned to my Heavenly Father to renew our relationship. In returning to Him, I discovered a new appreciation of my adoptive parents' love.

Do you sometimes feel as if you are sitting with Job? Assuredly, the rain falls on the just and unjust alike. Job lives righteously and thereby receives God's praise. Satan chides God into removing the hedge of protection and prosperity that surrounds Job. Unexpectedly and inexplicably, Job experiences destitution as he loses the entirety of his children and his financial and material possessions. Friends come to comfort Job in his misery. As they sit with him, questions emerge as to the underlying cause of Job's sudden reversal of fortune. Job's friends insist he has some unconfessed sin that if he were to admit and ask forgiveness for, his fortunes would return. Job's wife, in her agony and bafflement, cynically recommends that Job curse God and die. She sees no reason to continue living. Forty one chapters of arguably the most human and compelling book in the Bible, Job struggles with his feelings of being abandoned by Almighty God. Strikingly, Job asks, "Do you have eyes of flesh? Do you see as a mortal does?" (Job 10:4). As you survey the canvass of your life, what do you see? To date, have your experiences in love and work been a gorgeous mosaic of colorful relationships and brilliant jobs? Rather, has your life been a poster board collage of frightful clippings from gossip and tabloid magazines? Chances are your survey of your life creates a lingering question. Where was God? As you ask, you immediately relate with Job's grievous predicament. Has God abandoned you to life's chaos? What is the purpose in serving Him if He allows natural disasters and personal tragedies to befall you?

"If you are spiritual enough to ask God why He allows problems in your life, than you should be humble enough to also ask God why He allows blessings in your life."

The Psalter is another biblical witness who asks these difficult questions. Asaph boldly inquires whether God has forgotten Israel as the nation experiences a thorough and lingering national disaster. He yearns to be confident in God's love, character and faithfulness but the extent of Israel's anguish and God's extended silence when their collective existence appears in jeopardy undermine his hopes. Speaking for his people, Asaph courageously asks, "Will the Lord reject us forever, never again show His favor?" Further, "Has God's love ceased forever? Has the promise failed for all ages?" Disconsolate and inconsolable, the Psalter concludes "My sorrow is this; the right hand of the Most High has left us." Can you relate to Asaph's feelings? Do you continue to ask a very personal adaptation of his questions? Cumulative failure, in love and work, results in your autobiographical and unwritten version of Psalm 77.

NEVER FORGET YOUR PREVIOUS BLESSINGS

To resolve his dilemma, the Psalter recalls the mighty past deeds of God. He recounts God's enduring kindnesses to Jacob and Joseph during the famine in the land. Providentially, God allows Joseph's brothers to sell him into slavery as a means of preparing Joseph to be God's instrument for the preservation of God's chosen people during a ravenous famine. Through enslavement, false rape allegations, and lengthy imprisonment, Joseph realizes God's presence and graciously finds forgiveness toward his brothers in his heart. At the end of the book of Genesis, Joseph, in an act of wondrous graciousness, not only forgives his brothers, but explains how God's unfailing love and perfect purposes influence every circumstance. Asaph, in reflecting upon Joseph's story and subsequent divine deeds like the Exodus, wilderness years and Israel's arrival in the Promised Land, freshly appreciates God's unquestionable faithfulness. Psalm 86:10 says, "You alone are the God who did wonders; among the peoples you revealed your might." Reflection upon God's enduring reliability and kindness is a sure means of overcoming false feelings that He abandons you. If you look again at the canvass of your life, focus more intently upon the details. Hidden within both broad brushstrokes and minute finishes is God's incredible handiwork. For me, at the very moment that I thought He had abandoned me, He stood in the neonatal unit and arranged for me to experience love and nurture from two amazing people who understand that His love transcends biology, legacy and genealogy. Take a moment to consider the many ways in which God silently orchestrates your life's messiness and darkness toward a loving and hopeful outcome.

The prophet, Jeremiah, known as the young weeping preacher also offers comfort to anyone who believes God abandons him. Though he is young and possibly easily intimidated, Jeremiah obeys the Lord's orders to prophesy about the forthcoming destruction of Israel by the Babylonians. Needless to state, he does not gain any praise or popularity from the king and his advisers, specifically, nor the people of the nation, generally. They detest Jeremiah's words. In response to Jeremiah's obedience, the Lord allows the prophet's false imprisonment. Compounding Jeremiah's loss of freedom, the Lord directs the prophet to purchase land from a relative which Jeremiah will not be able to inhabit for seventy years. The land purchase symbolizes the length of Israel's exile in a foreign nation. The people of Israel react rather negatively when Jeremiah informs them that they will be away from home for that length of time. Nearly four generations of their children will be born and grow up away from the land of their forebears, history, literature, religion, and heritage. If anyone can assume that God abandons him to chaotic and reckless circumstances, assuredly Jeremiah can. Though he righteously follows God's directives, Jeremiah experiences isolation, rebuke, scorn and imprisonment. He pointedly and brilliantly asks, "Why is my pain unending and my wound grievous and incurable? You are to me like a deceptive brook, like a spring that fails," (Jeremiah 15:18). If you have been sad and depressed most of your life, particularly if you determine you are good and live an upright life, then you relate especially to Jeremiah's tough and provocative questions.

"We always have more than we deserve, but we always feel that we deserve more than we have." —Author unknown

Attempting to resolve the personal and philosophical question concerning whether God abandons you to life's daily chaos in turn requires that you ask tough questions of faith. Contrary to popular belief and practice in many churches, difficult questions create a pathway to authentic and relevant faith, which empowers and encourages you to face life's challenges with divine fortitude, grace, integrity and peace of mind. Parrot-like recitations of church clichés and traditional religious sayings do not equal a genuine reliance upon Almighty God. Actually, these phrases cloak entrenched fear and aimlessness. Additionally, asking perfectly polished and sparklingly theological questions hardly enables you to surmount daily adversities. As a pastor, I doubt being able to rehearse the problem of theodicy—the dilemma of prevalent evil in the world simultaneously existing with God's eternal presence—will practically explain the evil in your personal life. Still, you must reconcile God's goodness and faithfulness as you struggle with numerous challenges. Where is God in the midst of the painful, pervasive and bitter grief of Sister Deanna's mother, husband, siblings, and extended circle of family and friends as they wrestle with her sudden, unexpected, and inexplicable death two days after giving birth? Deanna only desired two things in life: marriage and motherhood. After four years of marriage, she becomes pregnant and dies within two days of delivering her son who will grow up without his beloved mother. Mr. Daniel will never know just how much she loved him. Do you encourage Sister Wilma to be confident though she just received a cancer diagnosis? How can she glorify God? What words of encouragement do we offer families whose debt burdens threaten their homes and stability? How do I counsel a fellow pastor as he undergoes a divorce when he has done nothing wrong? More personally, how will you overcome your feelings of lingering rejection and other emotional issues? Perhaps, the real theological questions are daily encounters with death, disease, debt, divorce and depression. Genuine faith asks hard questions and trusts Almighty God for trustworthy and applicable answers.

Another way to phrase the question is to ask, "Am I living a cruel joke?" Some devout churchgoers immediately will condemn the question as cynical and irreverent. Still, periodically, you want to know whether

God is humiliating rather than humbling me. Shakespeare's Macbeth offers an agonizing assessment relating to irony and incongruity in life. "Am I living a cruel joke?" That is a very practical, blunt way of asking the longstanding theological question about the disparity between God's existence and perpetual, collective and personal evil. If my biological parents deemed me as worthless as it relates to the time and commitment of rearing a child, and other people confirm their decision through numerous failed work and romantic relationships, then I must be the one in the dark. It feels as if everyone laughs at me as people consider my life to be a joke. I am the only one who fails to see that I am living and personifying a joke. Shakespeare ideally, perfectly and exquisitely expresses my sentiments. On the lips of Macbeth, he places these compelling words. *"Life is but a walking shadow, a poor player that struts and frets his hour upon the stage. And then I heard no more. It is a tale told by an idiot, full of sound and fury, signifying nothing,"* (William Shakespeare, Macbeth Act 5, Scene 5, Lines 20-25). Decades of anger, sadness and depression culminate in the heart wrenching feeling that your life is a story told by a dunce who smiles broadly and laughs uproariously as he communicates the details of your pain. Startlingly, those of us who dare to feel these hurtful sensations ask honestly, whether God sadistically watches our anguish and gleefully listens to fruitless prayers. He already knows that misery, disappointment and colossal failures will fill the hours of each of our earthly days. We pray and strive in vain. Is God humiliating me to humor Himself as He satisfies His sadistic impulses as the Sovereign of the Universe?

Has God rejected me, contrary to everything I learned previously? Were my Sunday school teachers and other religious persons who I encountered a part of a cosmic scheme to convince me to believe futilely? Lest you hasten to accuse me of cynicism because of the depth of my pain,

I equally hurry to note that many persons of "great" faith asked their own version of this question. Shortly after her death in 1997, *Time* magazine published a cover story about the questions of doubt and angst that plagued Mother Teresa for a considerable portion of her life. It seems as if even she thought that the world's entrenched poverty and unwillingness to correct it had eclipsed God. Martin Luther King, Jr.'s "Kitchen Experience," as recorded by David J. Garrow in his award winning biography, *Bearing the Cross: Martin Luther King, Jr. and the Southern Christian Leadership Conference*[4], arguably was the pivotal moment in his ministry. Handling yet another threatening phone call from an anonymous person in Montgomery, Alabama during the height of the bus boycott, King wondered whether he enjoyed God's blessing upon what historians and others label as the Civil Rights Movement. Though people labeled him as a master of suspicion, Malcolm X rightly articulated his inability to reconcile racism and Christianity. He refused to ignore the complexities of wrestling with inconsistencies of faith and reality. The noted atheist, the late Christopher Hitchens, was unable to reconcile his mother's suicide with the prevalence of commercial and collective religion, which demanded blind faith and obedience. Hitchens eloquently and vehemently espoused his personal disdain for organized religion. He forcefully advanced the position that religion poisoned everything, particularly the years of conflict, battle and death in the Middle East. A venerated nun who taught the world to see poor people for the first time, Mother Teresa wondered whether God opens enough human eyes to make a difference. Two prophetic preachers, a Muslim and a Christian, Malcolm X and Martin Luther King, Jr., forced American society to grapple with faith's incongruity. Is God a White racist? An atheistic intellectual (who confronted devoutly religious people about futility of faith when disciples resist the necessity of asking very hard questions), Christopher Hitchens shook disciples out of their smug complacency as he detailed their selfish fears and past crimes in the midst of God's unwillingness to intervene in human affairs. In their own ways, they ask whether God abandons anyone. Searching deeply within your heart, you will find your very private and personal words, which ask similar questions. Has Almighty God abandoned you?

"Even when you feel rejected, you are still loved by God."

GOD LOVES YOU ALL THE TIME

Resoundingly, I disagree with any notion that God rejects anyone. To overcome any feelings of rejection by God, first, you must honestly and unconditionally admit you have these emotions. As the recovery communities continue to teach anyone on a spiritual journey, the primary step in resolving any problem is a genuine willingness to admit it. Acceptance empowers you to defeat the problem as it no longer possesses the control and power that silence gives it. When held secretly in your mind and heart, fear of any type echoes like Goliath's booming voice on the battlefield. When you name a problem, you lessen its hold upon you as you face it directly. If you justifiably believe that God has forsaken you, you should pray. Second, ask the hard questions, as a person of faith, which naturally flow from the belief that God abandoned you. Zora Neale Hurston begins one of the chapters of her enduring literary work, *Their Eyes Were Watching God*[5], about the faith of common people with a subtle but provocative assurance. "There are years for questions and there are years for answers." The latter part of Hurston's idea about the complexities, contradictions and constant changes in the life of a person of faith recommends that you listen for answers to your questions. I believe that God welcomes difficult questions about His character, will, or actions. Questions allow Him an opportunity to respond. Third, apply the practical and pragmatic lessons that periods of fruitful prayer and meditation impart to you. As you act upon divine wisdom, you realize God's questionable faithfulness as the main denominator in your life. Incidences of luck and good fortune lessen as you attribute positive relationships and occurrences as evidence of divine favor. Moreover, you acquire daily discipline to rely upon internal intuition, "the still, small voice," through which your unfailingly loving Heavenly Father communicates His "good, pleasing, and perfect" will. Fourth, deeply desire maturity in faith as you progress in a more genuine relationship with God. Ask God to open the eyes of your mind and heart to enable you to see and feel Him in your everyday affairs. Ask for a mustard seed's size of willingness to trust and believe God is able to accomplish miracles in your life. One day, you will awake and know your anger, sadness and depression have lifted. You will know joy and freedom for the first time in your life. Faith in God emerges from a dynamic and vibrant relationship with Him.

Accordingly, I dismiss the concept of divine rejection of anyone. If you sympathize with any of the previously discussed biblical characters who experience the dark night of the soul, you can find solace in their relationships with God. From their direct experience of God's unfailing love, you can glean spiritual assets which will enable you to triumph over the cloud of negative emotions that lurk persistently in the background of your life. These biblical witnesses demonstrate that establishing and developing within a genuine relationship with God is the surest way to experience resurrection from the flawed notion that Almighty God rejects anyone. I pray you will seek Him with your whole heart and assuredly find Him. Within that relationship which will become your "ultimate concern," you will receive healing and wholeness.

"For God so loved the world that He gave His only begotten Son." —John 3:16

5 FEELINGS OF REJECTION BY ALMIGHTY GOD INTO POSITIVE FAITH

1. Inexplicable death of a loved one, particularly if the loved one was a victim of a crime, accident or unforeseen health crisis

2. Unfair loss of employment and underemployment

3. Health crisis

4. Perpetual and multiple adverse experiences

5. Incomplete understanding of God's love

5 STEPS OF FAITH WHEN FEELING REJECTED BY GOD

1. Prayer and other spiritual disciplines

2. Search the Bible for revelation.

3. Expand your understanding of God's unfailing love, undeniable faithfulness and limitless grace.

4. Self-evaluation — What, if any, role did you play in creating your circumstances and what does it reveal about your character?

5. Spiritual direction — Seek some type of counseling or assistance from a spiritual mentor or life coach who can encourage and empower you as you persevere through this difficult process.

REVIEW QUESTIONS

Do you believe that God is in control of everything that happens in your life?

☐ Yes

☐ No

☐ Sometimes

☐ Other: _____

_____

Has there ever been a time in your life where you felt as if God was not blessing you? If YES, please write out that time.

☐ Yes _____

_____

☐ No

Have you ever been MAD at God? If so, how did you respond?

☐ Did not continue to pray

☐ Did not go to church

☐ Did not read the Bible

☐ Other: _____

_____

In spite of how you may feel, do you realize and accept that your life is filled with more blessings than burdens?

☐ I believe that

☐ I sometimes question if that is true

☐ I believe it, but the burdens are too heavy

☐ Other: _____

_____

In one word, how would you describe your life? _____

_____

Have you accepted that the Love of God is unconditional and available to you?

☐ Yes I have

☐ I struggle with believing that God can love me in light of my past

☐ I believe it, but I wonder if I am being punished for some previous actions

☐ Other: _____

_____

If you feel as if God has not forgiven you for some things in your past, list them and then pray and ask to be delivered from the feeling of guilt because God has truly forgiven you.

_____

_____

_____

_____

_____

ENDNOTES

1   King, Jr., Martin Luther. Acceptance Speech of The Nobel Peace Prize in Oslo, Norway, December 10, 1964.

2   Swinton, John. *Raging With Compassion: Pastoral Responses to the Problem of Evil* (Grand Rapids, MI: William B. Eerdmans Publishing Company, 2007).

3   Kushner, Harold S. *When Bad Things Happen to Good People* (Garden City, NY: Anchor Books, 1978).

4   Garrow, David J. *Bearing the Cross: Martin Luther King, Jr. and the Southern Leadership Conference* (New York: Harper Collins, 1986).

5   Hurston, Zora Neale. *Their Eyes Were Watching God* (New York: Perennial Classics, 1998).

HEALING 7
YOU ARE RESTORED: SUSTAINING HEALING FROM REJECTION

"People, even more than things, have to be restored, renewed, revived, reclaimed, and redeemed." —Audrey Hepburn[1]

I just want to leave you with one thing to remember in this final chapter. Stop regretting your past! You can't change it, erase it, or deny it. I pray you experience each dawn as a new day of healing from rejection and progress toward wholeness. In this chapter, I offer suggestions and insight for sustaining your healing from abandonment and rejection. Envision awaking each morning and confidently affirming aloud the words of the Psalter, "This is the day that the Lord hath made and I will rejoice and be glad in it," (Psalm 118:24). As you resolve to experience new joys, mysteries and freedoms, you will offer gratitude perpetually throughout the day. Each day affords another opportunity to receive divine favor as you live the life you imagine. Every dawn increases your appreciation of your uniqueness and individuality as a child of God. Indeed, you are "fearfully and wonderfully made" in the image of Almighty God. There is nothing wrong with you. Each morning, you rise and look in the mirror. As you progressively and unconditionally accept the person whom you see, you equally attain definite healing from any past emotional, mental, psychological, spiritual, and relational pain. Rather than regretting the past and wishing you could alter it, utilize it as a source of healing and empowerment.

"Get on your mark! Get ready! Get set! Now take your life back and live it to the fullest."

Decide with God's help to utilize your past pain as an asset. My wife often tells me, "Baby, quit being embarrassed about things you had no control over." I have learned over time, that in the ruins of your past, you find materials for building a brighter and rewarding future. Past pain and suffering cultivate the quality of endurance. Applaud yourself; you did not faint or quit. Your perseverance over the years chiseled your core character. The sum of your experiences made you a person of hope. You can discard your unconscious need for negativity, sadness, anger, and depression. Drawing strength from your ability to endure, you now expect a brilliant, successful, and positive daily existence. You welcome joy, fulfillment, and peace of mind as it relates to love and work. God will assist and empower you as you use the lessons of your past to smash the patterns in your thoughts, choices, and character that propelled you to live comfortably with chaos, adversity, and pessimism. Circumstantially, God embeds opportunities for personal development and spiritual growth in each obstacle. Thus, serious reflection upon your past offers ironic, intuitive, and interesting answers to achieving the life you deeply desire. Ask God to help you develop strategies for redirecting and reframing your reflections on the past. How can you redeem any pain and suffering you experienced?

Cease letting the past blind-side you. Do certain memories still possess the power to make you cringe? If yes, you probably still suffer under the lash of guilt, regret, hidden mistakes, and secrets. I encourage you to share your pain and suffering with another person in addition to talking with your Heavenly Father. Those flashes of past errors lose their ability to make you cower when they cross your mind as you articulate them. When you name them, they lose their control over you. If you disappointed yourself by compromising your core values and contradicting your ethics, simply acknowledge your mistakes. When you do so, you remove anyone's ability to extort you, including your own mind and conscience. Your willingness to admit what you have done eliminates the possibility that anyone can humiliate you. If you lacked the courage to prevent being taken hostage in a relationship, sharing your experience with someone else usually helps that person and liberates you from your prison of hurtful memories.

BE HONEST WITH YOURSELF

Look closely at the facts of the past as they hold the tools for present and future growth. I imagine you assume responsibility for decisions and choices that were never yours. As a sick newborn baby with severe health problems, I was powerless to influence the decision of my biological parents. I could only do what new infants do; I could only love unconditionally those persons who nurtured and loved me. I was unaware of the complexity of life's most heart wrenching dilemmas. I could not have known whether they questioned their ability to rear me. Did they possess the character, compassion, and commitment to rear a sick child even if he were their son? Their decision, regardless of its authenticity and rationality does not define my intrinsic and inherent worth. For nearly a quarter of a century, I believed that it did. I saw myself as a seriously damaged and defected person about whom his parents did not care. As I wrongly assumed responsibility for their actions, I also falsely trampled upon the unconditional love of my adoptive parents. As I write and reflect, I resolve to evaluate my past with a clearer perspective of facts as they reveal insights for healing and growth. My understanding of God's love and genuine human love, as personified in my adoptive parents, expands as I reflect upon His providence. I am grateful for God's unfailing love, which presented me with the gift of my adoptive parents and their unconditional love. Had I remained angry, bitter, and resentful, I would not have been able to see clearly how God tailors His unfailing love to meet our needs in every situation. A close look at the past allows my mind and heart to grow in my conceptualization and practice of love. I hope you, too, find enlightening ways of healing and growing as you survey your past.

"Be true to thine self and you cannot be false to anyone." –Socrates

YOUR HURTS CAN BE SOMEONE'S HELP

Even though you may have had a very hurtful and difficult past, you can use your past to help other people. My primary purpose in writing this book is my heartfelt hope that you and anyone else who reads it finds faith, open mindedness, willingness, resolve, and hope to heal from abandonment and rejection. In turn, as you experience a greater sense of self-acceptance, you will be able to encourage and empower other broken, hurt, and damaged persons who desire what you have. Your past pains qualify you to help other people. You will not theorize because you have experiential knowledge. A widow is the absolute best person to offer comfort and reassurance to a woman who just lost her husband. A woman whose husband is still living can only imagine the depth and grief of a new widow. Similarly, an alcoholic with long-term sobriety is the best person to walk alongside another alcoholic with suggestions on how to attain and maintain sobriety. As an embittered adoptive son who thoroughly resented his biological parents for abandoning him and misguidedly shunned the love of his adoptive parents, I assure anyone who experiences any type of rejection that healing awaits anyone willing to work for it. God will resurrect you from rejection whether through termination, unrequited love or within your nuclear and extended family. As He recalls you to new life, He endows you with love, grace and peace to serve Him by sharing His message of revival with anyone entombed to rejection. Your past is one of the most valuable assets you have.

I found success despite my negative experiences with rejection. So now that you have read about my life, what will you do with your life? Will you continue to blame your past on someone else? Will you allow it to hold you hostage? Will you allow it to prevent you from enjoying your future? Will you accept your past and use it as an inspiration to become happy, joyous, and free? I now realize that my rough past equipped me to progress towards the life I lead. I thank God for transforming my painful past into a prosperous present and even more brilliant future. As your life has not followed a straight path of paved roads, you have been given God's grace to appreciate any blessings you receive. In gratitude for God's enduring kindness, you share your blessings by utilizing your story to equip someone who seeks inner healing and wholeness.

THE POWER OF EXPECTATION

Vanable Moody, in his book *The People Factor*[2], talks about the power of relationships and how they can move us forward towards our success or hold us hostage to our past. There are many relationships, when I look back in my life, which have caused me to become the person I am today. This includes both good and bad traits, some that I love and some that I am still trying to rid myself of. However, I have learned that when I surround myself with positive people, I can expect a great future. Let me ask you, "What do you expect in the future?" I ask this question to challenge you to consider how your past may determine your next divine assignment as you more fully discover your mission and purpose. Notwithstanding my past problems which I detail throughout this book, I always thought of ways to secure success. From encyclopedias, to lotions, to insurance, to telephone services, to products sold on infomercials, I probably sold everything you imagine. Early in my life, I determined I would have a bright future regardless of what I chose to do. I worked with every MLM company; still, I maintain an inactive affiliation with a prosperous company, Organo Gold. Beyond success in sales, I really strove for the success I desired and needed to assure me that brighter days lay ahead. Likewise, I encourage you to seek a promising future. If you expect success, you will attain it. Mysteriously, it emerges and evolves in many forms; sometimes success materializes in ways we least expect. In life, you usually receive what you expect. As you overcome your past pain and rejection, what are you looking for in your future?

"Live every day on purpose, and expect great things to happen to you. Whatever you expect is what your life will give you. What do you expect from your life?"

Surprisingly, my feelings and experiences with rejection prepared and empowered me for a great future. I could not and would not accept "NO" from anyone about anything. I changed every negative occurrence into a positive outcome. Allow me to share a few recollections of situations in which various people said "NO" to me and I transformed their refusal into opportunities for personal growth. In my junior year of high school, a teacher told me that I lacked the skills to compete in an essay contest. Needless to say, I rebuffed his words and did not accept his "polite and helpful" observation. Instead, I found the right persons to assist me as I wrote my essay. To that teacher's great amazement, out of two thousand entries from New York City students, my essay won! As a result, I became Commissioner of New York Police Department for a day; I still carry the honorary shield in my wallet. At the start of my senior year in an all-Black and Latino high school, as I began the college application process, a Caucasian guidance counselor told me that I was not smart enough to attend a four-year college. I simply laughed in response to his demeaning remark. Anyway, I applied and was accepted to a traditional four-year degree granting school. "Never allow small minded people to keep you from achieving big dreams." The college that I really wanted to attend initially rejected my application for admission. Since Morehouse College said "NO," I enrolled at Morris Brown College, a neighboring institution. After my freshman year, I walked over to Morehouse College admissions office and said, "You made a mistake on my application last year when you said 'NO,' so here is your chance to say YES." Within three years, I earned a bachelor's degree in Religion. With sweet irony and great relish, I later returned to my high school as the commencement speaker. The counselor who insisted that I was not smart enough to attend college sat on the stage BEHIND me as I prepared to deliver the Keynote Address. Prior to my graduation from Morehouse College, I was failing a mandatory Spanish course. I could not speak a lick of Spanish. I had already been accepted provisionally to Duke University for graduate school. My instructor in Spanish recommended that I drop the course because my highest grade was a 46. Still, I refused to drop the class. When I received my final grade, I discovered that I had passed the class. Since I knew he could not change the grade, I went to discuss it with him. He explained, "I passed you based upon your determination to succeed." It is my genuine hope with which I offer heartfelt prayers that you have a similar determination to heal from any type of rejection you have experienced. Finally, in early 2010, my beloved wife, who was then Danielle Marie Frank, told me "NO" to a relationship because I was not her type. However, two years later, November 2, 2012, at 6:00 p.m. to be exact, her "NO" became a forever "YES." I changed her last name from Frank to Carter. "No" is not a period. It may just be a comma in your life. Don't let the loud cry of "No" over crowd the God given cry of "Yes" in your life when it comes to your desires that you know you are able and willing to work to achieve.

At birth, my biological parents rejected me; however, look more closely at how my life unfolded despite being rejected. Almighty God gave me two of the greatest parents on Earth. I was healed of my physical sickness early in life. A loving extended family and an equally loving church family surrounded me. God extended His grace toward me and called me to share His message with people. By God's grace, I continually receive limitless kindnesses from countless people who show unimaginable favor towards me. I have been invited to offer keynote sermons at innumerable churches throughout the country. I travel extensively throughout the world. I lecture at colleges and universities. If all of that were not enough, I married one of God's most beautiful and blessed daughters. I marvel at God's handiwork in my life, particularly when I consider that I began my spiritual journey as a seriously ill and vulnerable infant whose biological parents were overwhelmed by the circumstances of my birth and thoroughly frightened by the prospect of rearing me. Undeniably, God resurrected me from rejection and recalled me to new life. Today, stop blaming your past and using it as a convenient excuse to escape your future. Decide that you will live boldly as you embrace each opportunity.

STOP COMPLAINING AND START THANKING

To reiterate the importance of gratitude, forgiveness, and acceptance of God's mysterious favor in your life, I wish to return to the conversation that I had with Dr. Ralph West at the Cigar Bar. You will recall that he sternly scolds me about wanting my biological parents to pay for their dastardly deeds of abandonment and rejection. I wanted them to feel the same pain I felt over the years of resolving the affects and effects of their decision. He quickly rebuked me and told me to leave the grave of my rejection and come forth into new life. Essentially, he told me to forgive my biological parents by considering just how difficult their choice might have been. It stands to reason that putting a child up for adoption is not a decision that a mother and father could make easily or quickly. As young people, they legitimately may have been overwhelmed by the prospect of rearing a special needs child with very limited financial, material and intrapersonal resources. Actually, I do not know what I would have done. I would like to believe that I could never have considered adoption in that instance, but I am not certain. To state otherwise, I would be sanctimonious and hypocritical. Empathizing with their fear, pain, and circumstances reasonably, practically, and legitimately equips me to forgive genuinely. In judging them and thirsting for revenge, I failed to consider the possible years of regret and second-guessing that they may have experienced. Did the holidays always feel complete to them as they saw an empty chair at the table? Did they judge themselves as bad people who failed at parenthood from the very beginning? Did they feel broken and inadequate? Did they think that God would punish them perpetually for their decision? These questions reassure me that no one makes such a pivotal decision as adoption without struggle. As I feel their pain, I find forgiveness in my heart. Accordingly, I suggest you begin to imagine the pain of the people who hurt you. In so doing, you will receive God's grace and personal willingness to forgive.

"In order to T-H-A-N-K, you first have to T-H-I-N-K."
—Joe Samuel Ratliff

Secondly, he urged me to become grateful. After all, I was adopted by two loving parents. I am thankful of the time and era that I was born in. At another time in American history, I would have been placed in an institution as an unwanted child. In the bleakest of possibilities, I may have been the victim of euthanasia by some well-meaning, but morally misguided person who determined that I had no intrinsic worth. Nevertheless, as God sowed the seeds of providence in my life as I lay in the neonatal unit, I escaped myriad unknown dangers and even possibly death. Moreover, I lived to actualize the divine gifts and abilities with which I was born. Regrettably, my biological parents' decision became a tomb in which I lived for nearly thirty years. Still, as Dr. West encouraged me, I eventually matured emotionally, personally, and spiritually to acquire gratitude for each aspect of my story. It strains incredulity to think that I would actually offer thanksgiving and praise to Almighty God for the pain that tormented me for three decades. Looking at the past through lenses of gratitude lessens the sting of pain and reveals God's mysterious ways.

Third, he insisted that I stop referring to my parents as my adoptive parents. He affirmatively stated that God gave Mr. Eugene and Mrs. Mary Carter as my parents and not my adoptive parents. "How would you like it if they referred to you as their adopted child?" I recall that I hated my father saying, "Steven, I love you as if you were my own son." Each time he said those words to reassure me of his love, he reminded me of the limitations that I saw in our relationship. His supposed reassurances served to further entomb me to my sadness, depression, and misery about being abandoned, rejected, and adopted. Nonetheless, he simply told me to accept unconditionally that God personified His unfailing love in my parents. His admonition helped me to understand the necessity of yielding my will to the will of God. As I heal from my pain, I appreciate God's mystical and magnificent orchestration in the midst of turmoil. His love, grace, and faithfulness redeem pain and suffering.

My summary of the conversation I had with Dr. West on that night reminds me of the importance of true friendships when embracing a process of emotional healing. Having someone with whom you can confide your deepest and darkest secrets and desires gradually eliminates the power of these emotions. As you progress towards inner healing and wholeness, you stand to gain strength, wisdom, and courage from another person who cares for you.

SPEAK WORDS OF POWER INTO YOUR LIFE

I believe in the power of words. The Bible posits that life and death reside in the power of the tongue (Proverbs 18:21). Words are very important as they reflect your inner thoughts and beliefs. What you say reveals what you think. An athlete who speaks fear and defeat usually fulfills those negative expectations. The reverse is also true. Positive and faith-filled words yield success and achievement. I no longer speak negatively about my experience of nearly three decades entombed to abandonment, fear, depression, and rejection. I now release such destructive thoughts and feelings. One of the ways in which I sustain my healing from rejection is the articulation of resurrection imagery and renewal language. I experienced rebirth in love as I more clearly understand God's unfailing love which transcends human descriptions and categories. Daily, God recalls me to new life and tells me to come forth irreversibly from the grave of rejection. I relocate my focus from the cemetery of sadness, anger, and depression to a new house where I live a happy, free and joyous life. Today, I wish to be in a right relationship with people. Thus, I strive for reconciliation in any broken relationships.

Practically speaking, just as I put aluminum cans and broken pieces of glass on the curb for recycling, I salvage defeat, failure, disappointment, and pain. Artists construct masterpieces utilizing thousands of pieces of shards. Average persons simply discard these pieces of broken glass as trash and unusable. Though they can no longer fulfill their original purpose, these pieces of shard can become more purposeful than ever if someone recycles them. Similarly, Almighty God redeems pain and suffering to direct us toward mission and purpose. To rejuvenate means to give new life. It is a fancy word for revival, the historical and traditional church term and annual event to breathe new life into weary, worn, and burned-out disciples. For one week, churches held nightly meetings centering upon enthusiastic and energetic preaching and prayer to motivate longstanding members to recommit to spiritual, numerical, financial, and other types of personal and collective growth.

"If you paid yourself for every negative thought you had about yourself or someone else, would you be poor or would you be rich?"

As someone progressively healing from rejection, rejuvenation emerges as I fearlessly, humbly, and tirelessly seek the life I imagine. As I leave the tomb of rejection, I embark upon limitless exploration. In the words of T. S. Eliot, "We shall not cease from exploration, and the end of all our exploring will be to arrive where we started and know the place for the first time."[3] In biblical imagery, the children of Israel, through

God's graciousness of the Exodus, leave their four hundred and fifty years of slavery in Egypt. They wander in the wilderness forty years; essentially going in a circle. As the older generation who retained vestiges of their enslavement in their minds and hearts dies, the younger generation at the end of the fortieth lap in the wilderness arrives at their original starting point. There, they are most prepared to cross the Jordan River into the Promised Land. Upon entering the Promised Land, they experience renewal of their heartfelt dreams and hope to live in the place "flowing with milk and honey" that God swore to them as an inheritance for their forbears' faithfulness and obedience. Likewise, if you trust God and follow His guidance as you leave the graveyard of rejection, He will not only heal you, but God will lead you to new mysteries, experiences, and joys.

Cultivating resilience is important to sustain healing from any type of physical or emotional injury. The human body regenerates healthy cells to support recuperation from surgery. These new cells replace old, damaged ones. Interestingly, the process of regeneration harnesses leftover, but usable energy from the old cells to make new ones. In other natural forces, resilience occurs when good fortune and natural law combine to harvest the riches of a disaster for the purpose of revitalization. A cresting river actually cleanses the river as the overflow helps on discarding debris that would poison the marine life and plants. Mudslides expose fault lines that developers would do well to avoid. In economic terms, hard cycles, such as recessions and inflation, serve the worthwhile purpose of closing outdated and outmoded businesses that did not grow with science, technology, and market forces. Personally, resilience develops within your character when you persevere to your ultimate breaking point without snapping. You acquire the elasticity of rubber, which bends and stretches to adjust to any challenge without breaking or dissolving. Healing from emotional pain is a dynamic and complex process which does not occur along the path of a straight line. Mostly, you zigzag as you progress. Resilience empowers you to absorb setbacks and experience detours without quitting.

YOU CAN GET YOUR LIFE BACK

Arguably, a resolve to heal is the primary step. "A journey of a thousand miles begins with one step."[4] If you have not already done so, stop and determine wholeheartedly that you will receive healing and wholeness by God's grace. If you do not resolve that you will heal, and thus enjoy new life, you will linger with the familiarity of the pain with which you are accustomed to living. Your resolution to enjoy a life free from pain requires a lifelong commitment as you reap the blessing and benefits of healing relative to seasons and situations in your life. Bereavement, termination, financial losses, and unrequited love are not one-time occurrences. They are cyclical events which often reignite smoldering ashes. With each incidence, your cumulative wisdom and resolve aids you in handling your circumstances and emotions without relapsing into the quicksand of sadness, anger, and depression. Your resolve to heal breaks the patterns in your consciousness, choices, and character that create resistance to your good and growth.

> "You are not reading this book by accident, you are reading it on purpose. The only question is, will you allow the purpose to be fulfilled in your life?"

A lover of classic cars delights in retrofitting these vehicles for current use. Once during a visit to Northern California, I observed the interesting phenomenon that many residents use older model and classic cars as their standard means of transportation. I am not sure whether automakers still manufacture some of these models. As I walked through the neighborhood on a morning stroll with my wife, I wondered whether using these cars presented more problems than conveniences. My niece, in response to a question, shared that many persons simply retrofitted modern "bells and whistles" to these classic cars. On the weekends, you can observe a guy installing a state-of-the-art Bose car stereo system in his 1950s Thunderbird. Another fellow enhances his Chevrolet Nova with new rims. Yet another person embellishes his Pontiac Firebird with new halogen headlights. Her insight helps me as I heal from my feelings of abandonment and rejection. I retrofit my evolving understanding of God's love as demonstrated in the gift of my parents to my mind, heart, and character. Internalizing His grace and kindness removes the decades of pain I endured. It replaces my anger and anxiety with forgiveness and hope. As you heal, retrofit your prayers, meditations, and insights to your past wounds as healing salve.

Fundamentally, daily develop and utilize resurrection language and images. Affirm each day that God calls you forth from the grave of abandonment and rejection to new life. Visualize the miracle of Lazarus' resurrection in a cemetery in Bethany more than two thousand years ago. Stand next to Jesus, the disciples and Lazarus' sisters, Mary and Martha. Hear Christ say, "Lazarus, come forth!" Substitute your name for his. Smell the stench of death. Hear the hungry and squealing vultures circling overhead hoping to scavenge a free meal. Look with amazement at the weather beaten tombstones. Feel the pain of grief and anger as Mary and Martha weep for their brother; believing his death was avoidable if only Jesus had come sooner. Consider your thoughts of anguish as you contemplate why God allows your pain and suffering when He has the power to prevent and nullify it. Feel the eeriness of silence as Jesus joins the sisters in weeping for Lazarus. Feel the utter sense of hopelessness and powerlessness as the Miracle Worker appears unable to surmount this current challenge. Possibly, you share that sentiment; your journey toward healing twists and turns over tough emotional and relational terrain. Various detours distract you. Aimlessness inevitably arises and in turn creates hopelessness. As you, nevertheless, return to that graveyard in Bethany, you directly witness Lazarus' resurrection. More especially, you hear the Lord instruct some bystanders to "take off his grave clothes." Your daily use of resurrection language equates with taking off your mental and emotional grave clothes of anger, fear, doubt, cynicism, and hopelessness. Proclaim new life! Affirm your daily resurrection. Say "I now live the life I imagine and my Creator gives me." I am serious! Take one second and say that to yourself. Go ahead!! I am going to wait for you to say it! Now that you said it, how do you feel? I can imagine you feel something great moving inside of you! That is what happens when you decide to leave your past and move towards your future, which is filled with favor and blessings from God above. Therefore, when you falter and lapse into negative thinking and words, and you will at various times, learn to reframe and redirect. Cancel the thought. Rephrase it. Announce your resurrection from rejection.

An authentic relationship with Almighty God is the foundation for self-acceptance, self-approval, self-expression, and self-love, which are the main indicators of resurrection from rejection. The Psalter supremely defines self-acceptance in Psalm 139:13-16. All people live as broken persons until they accept the person in the mirror as a unique child of God who does not need fixing. When I told one of my mentors that I was going to lose weight and get in shape, he said these words to me,

"Great son, but make sure you are doing it for yourself and not someone else." Then he said something to me that has motivated me in a major way, he said, "Get in shape so that you can stay around to continue to spread the power of the Word of God." In other words, make better decisions for yourself, and others will be blessed by the decision you made to improve your life. Can I help you with something? Thanks for giving me permission. You owe it to other people to help yourself become a better YOU! Each of us acquires self-actualization within an interdependent relationship with God as divine and personal attributes and abilities unfold with daily, practical and concrete acts of service to humankind. Genuine spirituality is the most effective means of sustaining healing from rejection. The practice of daily spiritual disciplines inclusive of self-evaluation, prayer, affirmations, meditations, Bible study, imaging, visualization, and daily devotions are the means of grace to heal from past pain and persevere toward a new life.

"YOU are the greatest YOU that YOU could ever be, so decide today to be happy and content with being YOU and stop worrying about others who do not accept YOU."

As I am grateful eternally for your purchasing and reading this book, I keep a deep desire for you. I hope you take away one fundamental thought from this book. You can be whole! Greatness is ahead of you. However, you have to welcome it. As it relates to adoption, all of us were lost and have been adopted by a loving God and into a loving family. I am happy to be a Christian who respects all faiths. My faith reminds me of God's unconditional love and acceptance of me. I pray you live with knowledge of God's unconditional love for you. If nothing else offers you a reason for living and painstakingly pursuing healing, God's love does. Embrace His love and thereby find healing.

FAMOUS PEOPLE WHO WERE ADOPTED/REJECTED

When I was doing my research, I wanted to learn about some others who were adopted at birth. I was surprised when I googled and discovered that so many people succeeded in spite of their adoption reality. I want you to look at this list and tell yourself, "If they can succeed, so can I." The site from where I received these names was:

www.americanadoptions.com/adoption/celebrity_adoption

People such as *Marilyn Monroe (Actress), Dave Thomas (Founder of Wendy's), William Jefferson Clinton (Former United States of America President), John Lennon (Singer), Nelson Mandela (Former President of South Africa), Babe Ruth (Baseball Legend), Michael Bay (Director of the movie Transformers), Jesse Jackson (Civil Rights Leader), Richard Burton (Actor), Faith Hill (Singer), Steve Jobs (Founder of Apple), Eartha Kitt (Actress), Edgar Allan Poe (Writer), Jamie Foxx (Actor), Eleanor Roosevelt, Sheryl Crow (Singer), Tom Cruise (Actor), Oprah Winfrey (Talk Show Host), Angelina Jolie (Actress), Brad Pitt (Actor), Bruce Willis (Actor), Sandra Bullock (Actress), Meg Ryan (Actress), Les Brown (Motivational Speaker), Nat King Cole (Singer), Greg Louganis (Olympic Gold Medal Driver), Malcolm X (Human Rights Activist), Tom Monaghan (Owner, Domino's Pizza), Moses (Biblical Character), Michael Reagan (Son of Former United States of America President, Ronald Reagan), Nancy Reagan (Former United States of America First Lady), Newt Gingrich (Politician), John Hancock (United States Founding Father), Gerald Ford (Former United States of America President), Alonzo Mourning (NBA Player) and many more who have succeeded against all odds.*

Although these are just a few, this showed me one thing that I want to share with you. That is, if others can succeed in spite of their beginnings, so can you. If you have been blessed with life, don't waste it being mad at your start, just focus on how you will finish your life. It matters not how we start, it only matters how we finish. I hope that you will finish your life with a story and legacy that will offer encouragement to others who may struggle with issues beyond their control. Take charge and decide today, I am going to succeed no matter what it takes!

"What was taken by force, can only be restored by force." –Gamal Abdel Nasser[6]

REVIEW QUESTIONS

Are you ready to rise above your pain of rejection and walk into your future blessings?

☐ Yes I am

☐ I am, but I am scared

☐ I am, but I am comfortable

☐ No, I am not ready

What are three things you will commit to doing that you know will improve your life?

I will _____

I will _____

I will _____

Who are two people in your life who can help you with being accountable? You have to call them and let them know that you are depending on them for support in your process?

Full Name: _____

_____

Full Name: _____

_____

In what ways will you help others who are feeling rejected as a result of you improving yourself?

_____

_____

_____

What is your biggest fear about starting this process towards healing?

_____

_____

_____

Since you know that your life is blessed, what are 5 things that you can commit to stop complaining about? As of today, I will no longer complain about....

_____

_____

_____

WHENEVER YOU FEEL DISCOURAGED, SIMPLY SAY THIS TO YOURSELF....

"Regardless of my past, I am destined for greatness and I will no longer allow my fears to hold me hostage. Today is a new day for me to receive new blessings. I welcome all of my blessings and I cast away all of my fears. I can do all things through Christ who strengthens me"

ENDNOTES

1   Ferrer, Sean Hepburn. *Audrey Hepburn: An Elegant Spirit* (New York: Atria Books, 2003, p.217).

2   Moody, II, Vanable H. *The People Factor: How Building Great Relationships and Ending Bad Ones Unlocks Your God-given Purpose* (Nashville, TN: Nelson Books, 2014).

3   Eliot, T. S. "Little Gidding" *The Four Quartets* (New York, Harcourt Books, 1943).

4   Lao Tzu, *Tao Te Ching*, Chapter 64.

5   Nasser, Gamal Abdel as quoted in Sami Al Jundi and Jen Marlowe, *The Hour of Sunlight: One Palestinian's Journey from Prisoner to Peacemaker* (New York: Nations Books, 2011, p.47).

INSPIRATIONAL MESSAGE OF HOPE

This message is written from a Christian perspective as a result of my faith beliefs. Regardless of your faith belief, the principles in this message can be applied to your life and you can gain healing as you journey towards your recovery from the feeling of rejection.

RESURRECTION FROM REJECTION

Scripture: Acts 13:51

"So they shook the dust off their feet because of rejection, and went on to another city."

INTRODUCTION

Rejection is a real reality of life. We don't like it, don't understand it, and wish we could avoid it. Sometimes we are rejected by family, friends, co-workers, lovers, and even church members. Rejection is not just for the under-class, uneducated, or uninformed. Every person has felt the sting of rejection. Perhaps you were rejected by the girl you tried to talk to, the father who left you and your mother with no explanation, the spouse that abandoned you because of another lover, the church members who acted holier than thou, or even feeling rejected by your own self because of insecurities that you have not dealt with. The truth is that rejection is real, hurtful, destructive, discouraging, and can be lethal if not dealt with in a proper way.

Allow me to be open and real with you. As you have read in this book, more than 20 years of my own life I lived with the lethal reality of feeling rejected. As a result of those feelings, I found myself acting ugly towards people, never allowing people to love me or allowing myself to love someone. I pretended to be who I was not in an attempt to make up for insecurities of my own, all because I felt rejected by my birth parents who left me for dead in a hospital with no hope and no letter to explain their departure. I masked my rejection issues with degrees, preaching engagements and name dropping. I lived in a bubble, even when it appeared that I was open and honest. Rejection was so real to me until I was unable to become the man that God wanted me to be, all because I was looking for healing in unhealthy ways. However, I have learned that regardless of your past, regardless of your pain, and regardless of your position; you can heal from rejection if you genuinely desire to become all that God has called you to be.

In this lesson we find some disciples who were preaching the Gospel message of Jesus Christ, and they were preaching it to some people who did not want to hear it or see them. They were preaching to people who thought they already knew the right answer, and as a consequence, they rejected the disciples and rejected the message. The Disciples, who did not like the feeling of rejection, became discouraged, despondent and almost defeated. However, before they gave the benediction to their testimony, they received some encouragement to help them remain upbeat when they were feeling beat-down. I want to share these words of encouragement with you to help you get over whatever rejections you may feel in your own life. The lessons you receive you can apply to any area of your life where you are feeling rejected. You can apply in your home, on your job and amongst your friendships.

1, PEOPLE DO NOT REJECT YOU, THEY ONLY REJECT WHAT YOU REPRESENT

My parents did not reject me; they rejected the sickness and the responsibility that came with keeping me. **Therefore, I understand now in my 30s, I was never a rejected person; I was only a rejected responsibility.** Likewise, the people who were listening to the disciples did not reject the disciples; they rejected the commandments that the disciples were teaching. They knew that if they received their words, they would have to change their lives. Therefore, it was easier for them to reject the words than it would have been for them to redefine themselves. Which means that when people reject you, accept it, as they are rejecting the responsibility that is attached to being connected to you.

"People never reject you. They only reject the responsibility that comes with being connected to you." –Author unknown

2, WHEN PEOPLE REJECT YOU, GOD REDIRECTS YOU

My biological parents rejected me, but God redirected me to two loving parents who gave me the best life that I could have ever dreamed of. This means that whenever you are rejected, God will always redirect you to something or someone better. Rejection usually comes before elevation. That's what happened in this story. The disciples were rejected, but they were told to go to another city that would hear what they had to say. In essence, God is saying don't spend time trying to convince people to accept you or what you have to offer; instead, move on toward people who want to accept you and your gifts. Life is too short to worry yourself over people who are not receptive of you. Stop making people a priority who only make you an option. Ask God to order your steps to people and places where you and your gifts can be received.

FINALLY, # 3, YOU MAY BE REJECTED BY PEOPLE, BUT YOU ARE NEVER REJECTED BY GOD

Because God Loved me so much, as with Abraham, He had a ram in the bush. There is nothing you can do to cause God to stop loving you. There is no sin that is more powerful than His grace and mercy. He forgave David for adultery, Moses for murder, Noah for being drunk, Peter for denying Him, Jonah for disobeying Him, Thomas for doubting Him, Paul for talking against Him, and the Roman Soldiers for crucifying Jesus. Which means, if He did not reject them for all of their sins, then He will never reject you for any of your failures in life. His Word says, "…while we were still in our sins, Jesus died for us," (Romans 5:8). That means that when you were living wrong, He died right so that you would one day be able to live right in spite of your living wrong. Hold your head up, stick your chest out, and when people reject you, don't sweat it. Just remember, they also rejected Christ.

Be encouraged today and know that you are somebody, and you do not need validation from any man, woman, boss, co-worker, church member, pastor, deacon or trustee. God made you and God will never make or create something or someone who He will not love. You are not rejected. You are fully accepted and loved by God. Be encouraged on today.

52 WEEKLY QUOTES
TO POST ON YOUR SOCIAL MEDIA

As we are focusing on creating a movement for people to rise above their feelings of rejection, please use the hashtag #NoRejection when posting comments from this book or making reference to Steven Carter. Thanks a lot.

1. "People Never Reject You. They Only Reject the Responsibility that Comes with Being Connected to You." #NoRejection

2. "When You Realize that You Are Accepted by the God Who Created EVERYONE, Then You Cannot be Defined, Limited or Deformed By Rejection from ANYONE." #NoRejection

3. "Acceptance of Self Will Always Free You from the Bondage of Rejection by Someone Else." #NoRejection

4. "Sometimes You Cry Because You Were Rejected By Someone You Really Did Not Want to Be Connected To. You're Just Mad You Didn't Initiate the Rejection." #NoRejection

5. "You Are Only Rejected By Individuals Who Never Took the Time to Get to Know Who They Were Rejecting. Their Loss." #NoRejection

6. "The Key to Success is Learning to Outlive Your Rejection Experiences. The People Who Can Live with Multiple Rejections in Life, Are the People Who Will Meet the Greatest Success In Life." #NoRejection

7. "If You Were Never Rejected By Someone You Thought Was Good for You, You Would Have Never Had the Chance to Be Accepted by Someone Who God Knew Would Be Great for You." #NoRejection

8. "It Is Better to Accept Yourself and Be Rejected By Everyone Else, As Opposed to Being Accepted by Everyone Else and Rejecting Yourself." #NoRejection

9. "Deal with Your Painful Past Memories NOW, before Your Painful Past Memories Interrupt Your Promised Future LATER." #NoRejection

10. "If You Are Afraid of Rejection, You Are Not Prepared for Success." #NoRejection

11. "Rejection May Cause You To Cry Now, But Reflection on Your Rejection Will Make You Rejoice Later." #NoRejection

12. "If You Can't Handle Being Rejected By Small Minded People, You Will Never Be Able to Receive Acceptance from Big Minded People." #NoRejection

13. "The Door to Your Future Is Locked by the Pain of Your Past. Only You Have the Key to Open it and Let Yourself Out, How Long Will You Stay In Your Room of Rejection?" #NoRejection

14. "Quit Focusing On People Who Accept Some of You, And Build Relationships with Those Who Accept All of You." #NoRejection

15. "I am Not Crying Because I Was Rejected by You; I am Crying Because I Can't Believe that I Wanted to be Accepted by You." #NoRejection

16. "You Could Not Control How You Were Born, But You Can Control How You Live." #NoRejection

17. "Rejection Doesn't Define You, It Only Develops You." #NoRejection

18. "Until You Stop Rejecting Your Present Reality, You Will Never Develop Your Future Potential." #NoRejection

19. "Rejection is God Trying to Blow Out a Certain Fire In Your Life. Depression is You Blowing the Flame Trying to Keep It Lit." #NoRejection

20. "When You Are Rejected by Someone, Simply Say, 'Thank You for Releasing Me to Live My Life.'" #NoRejection

21. "Quit Allowing Dead People Who Rejected You In Your Past To Have Power Over Your Life from their Grave—Forgive and Live Your Life." #NoRejection

22. "Stop Looking for Acceptance from Individuals Who Have Not Accepted Themselves." #NoRejection

23. "Rejection is God's Way of Saying, "I Did Not Create You to Be Accepted by Everyone"." #NoRejection

24. "If Jesus was Never Rejected by the Roman Government, We Could Have Never Been Accepted by our Heavenly Father. Thank God for Rejections in Life." #NoRejection

25. "You Can Live Better with Truthful Rejections than You Can with False Acceptance." #NoRejection

26. "Quit Allowing Rejection from Your Earthly Father to Overpower Your Acceptance from Your Heavenly Father." #NoRejection

27. "TODAY is the last day that I am feeling depressed, discouraged, destroyed or damaged. I am living my life of acceptance and burying my feelings of rejection." #NoRejection

28. "Therapy Is Not a Sign That You Are Crazy. It is a Sign That You Love Your Life Enough to Properly Process Your Past Pains." #NoRejection

29. "You Can Only Walk In Acceptance By God When You Are Able to Handle Rejection by Man." #NoRejection

30. "The Reality is That Rejection Is Only Temporary. The Danger Is When You Make it Eternal." #NoRejection

31. "People Who Reject Your Failures Early In Life, Are Only Making Room for Others to Accept Your Successes Later In Life." #NoRejection

32. "Quit Holding On to Someone Who Doesn't Want to Stay. Let Them Go." #NoRejection

33. "You Will Never Arrive In Your Accepted Future If You Keep Looking at Your Rejected Past." #NoRejection

34. "A Mind of Self-Acceptance will Never Make Room for Little Minds of Rejection." #NoRejection

35. "If You Are Loved and Accepted by a Big Minded God, Do Not Give Rejection Power from Little Minded People." #NoRejection

36. "In Order to Reach Your Mountain of Acceptance, You Must Walk through Your Valley of Rejection." #NoRejection

37. "Successful People Live THROUGH their Rejections. Unsuccessful People Live IN Their Rejections." #NoRejection

38. "The Person Who Rejected You Last Year, Only Made Room for the Person Who Accepted You This Year." #NoRejection

39. "If I Were Never Rejected By my Biological Parents, I Would Have Never Been Loved by my Adopted Parents." #NoRejection

40. "People Who Reject You Now Don't Understand That, Like Wine, You Only Get Better With Time." #NoRejection

41. "I Would Rather You Reject Me Now, Before I Wise Up and Reject You Later." #NoRejection

42. "I Will Never Allow You to Make Love to Some of Who I am, If You Refuse to Accept All of Who I am." #NoRejection

43. "Don't Expect to Get What's Underneath My Blouse & Skirt, If You Choose to Reject What's Inside My Head & Heart." #NoRejection

44. "If I Never Learned How to Live with Rejection from Others, I Would Have Never Learned How to Live with Acceptance by Self." #NoRejection

45. "Rejection from Humans Will Sometimes Hurt. However, Acceptance from God Will Always Heal." #NoRejection

46. "You Only Rejected The Me That I Showed You. Thank God I Did Not Show You All of Who I Am." #NoRejection

47. "You May Fall Asleep Feeling Rejected By a Person, But When You Wake Up, That's Proof That You Have Been Accepted By God to Live In Spite of Your Rejection." #NoRejection

48. "Love Those Who Reject You, But Learn to Love Them at a Distance." #NoRejection

49. "If People Only Accept You When Others Accept You, Than Be Prepared for Them to Reject You When Others Reject You." #NoRejection

50. "I Can Handle Someone Who Rejects Me Publicly Better Than I Can Handle Someone Who Only Accepts Me Privately." #NoRejection

51. "Whenever You Choose to Live In Your Past, You Have Just Made the Decision to Die In Your Future." #NoRejection

52. "Rejection In Your Life is a Chapter. Rising Above Your Rejection Is the Book." #NoRejection

SUGGESTED READINGS

The People Factor, *Vanable Moody*

12 Steps to Learning How to Handle Rejection, *Slim Phatty*

God Loves You, *David Jeremiah*

Six Battles Every Man Must Win, *Bill Perkins*

Dare to be True, *Mark D. Roberts*

My Life Is Not My Own, *Bill Bright*

Healing the Shame that Binds You, *John Bradshaw*

No More Excuses, *Tony Evans*

Attitude is Everything, *Jeff Keller*

The Winning Attitude, *John C. Maxwell*

Dare to Drop the Pose, *Craig Groeschel*

The Slight Edge, *Jeff Olsen*

Soul Fitness, *Frederick Haynes, III*

Could You Not Tarry One Hour?, *Larry Lea*

Everybody's Normal Till You Get to Know Them, *John Ortberg*

Don't Waste Your Life, *John Piper*

Eat that Frog, *Brian Tracey*

10 Lies about God, *Erwin W. Lutzer*

If the Church Were Christian, *Philip Gulley*

Finding Fullness Again: What the Book of Ruth Teaches About Starting Over, *Ralph D. West*

Twenty Things Adopted Kids Wish Their Parents Knew, *Sherrie Eldridge*

Don't Take It Personally: The Art of Dealing with Rejection, *Elayne Savage*

Outlier: The Story of Success, *Malcolm Gladwell*

God's Creative Power for Healing, *Charles Clapp*

Wounded Healer, *Henri Nouwen*

Dialogue with My Daughters, *Jeffrey Johnson*

Enemies of the Heart: Breaking Free of the Four Emotions that Control You, *Andy Stanley*

Becoming a Couple of Destiny: Living, Loving, and Creating a Life that Matters, *Joseph Walker*

Breaking the Chains of Low Self-Esteem, *Marilyn Sorensen*

Adapt: Why Success Always Starts with Failure, *Tim Harford*

You Are Going to Fail! So Get Over It, *James Weaver*

It Happens After Prayer: Biblical Motivation for Believing in Prayer, *H. B. Charles, Jr.*

God Wants You to Grow: How to Live Beyond Your Limitations, *William D. Watley*

ABOUT THE AUTHOR

Steven Eugene Carter is a native of Brooklyn, New York. He serves as Lead Pastor of Mount Ararat Church of Brooklyn, New York. He earned degrees from **Morehouse College** of Atlanta, Georgia, and **Duke University** of Durham, North Carolina. He travels the country as a sought after speaker & lecturer. He is happily married to the former Mrs. Danielle Marie Frank. They presently reside in Bayonne, New Jersey.

BOOKING INFORMATION

If you desire to have Steven Carter as a Keynote Speaker or Lecturer, you may email: steven@steven-carter.com

Stay Connected with Steven Carter

Facebook /stevencarterny

Instagram @StevenCarterNY

Twitter @StevenCarterNY

Hashtag: #NoRejection

Webpage: www.steven-carter.com

Blog: www.stevencarterny.com